RealtyPro Advisor

Success Series

Learn the Lingo of Houses

2016 Version

Reference of Real Estate Terms for Today's Industry Professionals

by Regina P. Brown

www.RealtyProAdvisor.com

LEARN THE LINGO OF HOUSES

Learn the Lingo of Houses 2016 Version: Reference of Real Estate Terms for Today's Industry Professionals

~~~

2016 Edition, January 2016

Copyright © 2016 Regina P. Brown

All rights reserved.

~~~

ISBN: 978-1-62546-011-0 (paperback)

ISBN: 978-1-62546-012-7 (digital book)

Author and Designer: Regina P. Brown

Illustrator: Tanya Leontyeva

Cover Graphic: Sudipta Dusgupta

Editor: Miriam Fajardo

Publisher: Queen Bee Publisher Inc., Cheyenne WY

~~~

Summary: This book is designed for real estate sales agents, home stagers, property managers, interior designers, and home inspectors. It is a reference manual with hundreds of real estate industry phrases defined in one handy guide. Illustrations are included with the jargon. Appendix includes glossary of transaction terms and a chart with acronym definitions.

Topics: real estate, house, home, features, jargon, definition, glossary, terms, lingo, reference. Non-fiction.

ENDORSEMENT

by Marguerite Crespillo

As a trainer and coach to many top producing agents, I often get asked how career professionals can increase their product knowledge of houses. Up until now, there was no resource that was a single source of terms and jargon used in our industry to which I could direct them. New agents had to learn through on-the-job experience.

Now, after being a part of more than 3,000 closed real estate transactions over a career spanning 23+ years as a real estate brokerage president, I realize there so much to know and learning is a continual process. I sometimes think I have seen everything and then I come across a wonderful resource like this book — it makes me amazed at how much I still need to continue learning.

Discover the wealth of knowledge contained within the pages. This "Learn the Lingo" guide explains features found in gourmet kitchens, luxury bathrooms, historic vintage houses, rural properties, GREEN homes, and so much more. For agents broadening their skill set to encompass luxury homes and compete for high-end listings, this book is must-have gem.

The best thing about this guide is it creates a short cut to hundreds of hours spent researching the great information you now have at your fingertips. This truly should be REQUIRED reading of everyone in the real estate industry!

By having the book handy, like a real world real estate dictionary, will definitely give you the edge needed in today's competitive market. Keep a copy in your car, at your desk, by your bedside... I am serious!

Marguerite Crespillo
Chief Master Facilitator and Trainer
MasterClass Real Estate Academy
www.MasterClassRealEstateAcademy.com
Realtor® and licensed by CalBRE

DEDICATION

Dedicated to all of the hard-working real estate professionals who chose this humble, yet noble career to help advance the American Dream of homeownership.

A whole-hearted thank you to my Lab Coat Agents colleagues who contribute generously from their wealth of knowledge and especially to the Admins who serve tirelessly 'round the clock to elevate the standard of professionalism.

To my REALTOR® friends and associates: Kudos for making the effort to develop your career and to advance yourself professionally. You are earning consumer trust while raising the standard for our industry! Here's to your success.

With deep gratitude to my friends at the San Diego Association of REALTORS® who graciously published my first article series. I appreciate your confidence in me as an author and I share your vision of delivering extraordinary value to members.

SUMMARY

We hear a lot of unusual "house" words in our real estate industry, and sometimes we don't understand all of them. Often called jargon or lingo, we learn these buzz words in the field and on the job.

Wouldn't it be great to have a reference book with all of the real estate industry "catch phrases" in one handy guide? You can impress your clients with your knowledge of the right words at the right time. That's why we compiled all the terms you need to know, plus more, into this comprehensive reference manual.

This guide is specially designed for real estate sales agents, home stagers, property managers, interior designers, and home inspectors. Even if you've been in the real estate business for decades, you're guaranteed to learn new terms!

We define each term so it's easy to understand. It's like a "house" lingo mobile crash course. You won't find a more all-inclusive guide anywhere else. Our comprehensive guide book reflects years and years of product knowledge in the real estate industry.

Our 2015 version of this handy "lingo" guide lists house features the following sections: architectural styles, gourmet kitchens, luxury bathrooms, lighting, windows, fences and gates, outdoor yard structures, historic / vintage features, doors, tile, roof architecture, and "green" eco-conscious houses.

How is this book improved from the 2014 version? We doubled the content, with a total of over 400 terms! We included links to color photos of the terms on our pinterest page — check the link at the beginning of each chapter. Lastly, and most importantly, we added hundreds of custom hand-drawn illustrations that help explain each term so you can grasp the meaning quickly and easily.

As a bonus, we included an appendix in the back of the book. Refer to that special section, which contains a glossary of transaction terms AND a chart with acronym definitions. Enjoy learning the lingo and boost your career!

Table of Contents

INTRODUCTION

When I earned my real estate license way back in 1988, I was bursting with excitement. After all, I had prepared myself by completing 8 college level real estate courses with high marks, culminating in 2 Associate degrees: one in real estate and another in small business management. A real estate career sounded simple. Next, I studied for the California real estate licensing exam and passed it with ease... so of course my new career would be a breeze, right?

WOW, was I ever wrong about that. I found out the real world of real estate sales is an utterly unique experience, and most of my on-the-job learning was not covered by book knowledge. Although it became a basic cornerstone of my career, the college education did not prepare me for the real field work required in real estate.

In everyday practice, we must know about building construction, contracts, inspections, disclosures, appraisals, decorating and design, architecture, contracts, negotiating, building codes, title vesting, property valuation, probates, county building permits, zoning, contracts, escrows, mortgage loan requirements, insurance, a myriad of new laws... and did I mention contracts?

Then with the downward market cycles, we are obligated to learn about short sales, REOs, foreclosures, bankruptcies, and BPOs. On top of that, we have to spend an enormous effort marketing listings (and ourselves) to continually obtain new clients, while simultaneously staying ahead of technology and keeping up with training... and we must do all of this with a smile and a great attitude (and of course high ethics)!

Not only was there a LOT to learn, but I found my job both interesting and challenging because of the variety: every house was different, every buyer and seller had different needs, and every transaction had different obstacles. I immersed myself in the real estate world and absorbed as much as I could. While (thankfully) I had mentors to guide me along, much of my accumulated knowledge was acquired by observing, researching, and participating. That's why I stay connected to our industry resources such as the local REALTOR® Associations. Even today, I am continually learning new things within the real estate industry from seasoned pros.

It's taken me 26 years to learn, collect, and compile this resourceful "crash course" of real estate terms. I wrote this book to help you become knowledge and gain expertise much faster than I did.

To compare a variety of color illustrations for these terms, visit our Pinterest page at:

http://www.pinterest.com/realtyproadvisr

In this comprehensive reference manual, you can new discover terms in each section, or use it as a reference guide when needed. Enjoy our handy book and have fun learning the lingo of houses!

1. Architectural Styles

View sample illustrations on our pinterest board:
http://www.pinterest.com/realtyproadvisr/architectural-styles-of-houses

American architectural styles reflect our vibrant cultures, vast geographic areas, and time-forgotten eras. Discover the rich heritage of the most popular home types you may encounter in your real estate career. Designs and colors were influenced by local building materials available, and adapted to regional landscapes.

Ever wonder how to distinguish a Cape Cod from a Colonial? A Mission from a Mediterranean? A Prairie from a Pueblo? Keep reading and unravel the mysteries of house architecture designs.

A-Frame

This contemporary style is characterized by its easy-to-recognize pointed triangle roof which resembles an "A". This all-seasons house is designed to capture sunlight with large windowed fronts and backs that overlook lake views. The large decks accommodate vacationing family and friends. It was most popular during the 1960s and 70s in resort areas, such as mountain retreats and ski getaways. The interior is open with a fireplace, bedroom, and loft nestled into the attic. This steep sloping roof is specially designed for snowy climates and the house is generally designed to fit in with its natural surroundings using existing materials and tan / brown hues.

Bungalow

Identify this style by its low horizontal roof, earthly colors, front porch, and wood siding. It's a small, simple space with a fireplace focal point. The living room opens to the dining room with built-in wooden furniture such as bookcases, window seats, buffets, and sideboards. The interior includes plaster walls and is characterized by wood floors and chair rails, stained glass windows, and artisan lighting fixtures. This style, developed from the Arts and Crafts era influence, was popular in the 1920's. Closely related is the California Bungalow that borrows the colonial Spanish motif.

Cape Cod

Look for a steep roof, gray wood shingles or clapboarding, no front porch, and a white picket fence. Other identifying features include a brightly colored front door with intricate carvings and an ornament; white trim and window shutters; airy clean-look white paint on doors, crown molding, and cabinets which sharply contrast with the wood floors. Walls are painted to reflect the Cape Cod colorful seaside, echoing the blue ocean, tan sand, and glowing orange/reddish sunsets. Based on the colonial lifestyle of the early pilgrim settlers, the simple functional design originates from 17th century New England. Exteriors are characterized by broad low frame steep sloping roofs, symmetrical pitched style with a front door in the middle, and windows with shutters on each side. Native woods such as cedar shingles were used frequently, along with oak/pine hardwood flooring. Interiors may have a hallway, parlor, upstairs left and simple open floor plan. Think of: Martha's vineyard style.

Circular

Octagon, silo, and round houses are examples of circular architectural style. They are eco-friendly and highly energy efficient. Circular styles are known for withstanding tornados and hurricanes because their design offers protection against the harsh elements. They are ideally suited for country living where views abound, with large windows boasting panoramic views. Home builders can buy a "kit" and build it on site from Deltec.com, the most popular DIY round house. Related styles are the geodesic domes and cone shapes.

Colonial

Exteriors are narrow and tall, boxy rectangular structures, with a natural wood-look. Other identifying features are muted grays & earth tone colors, vertical tall doors and windows, and multi-panel windows. This simple and sensible style from the early American settlers and pioneers has narrow, non-decorative trim which reflects the conservative craftsman style. From the basic colonial style developed French Colonial, Spanish Colonial, Dutch Colonial and Georgian.

Contemporary

This modern, minimalist style is known for its striking artistic asymmetrical roof lines. Featuring boxy picture windows, the "industrial" look outside, and large flexible living areas inside. This eye-catching design offers a break from the cookie cutter tract home because each home is uniquely custom designed. Closely related to the Art Deco and Mid-Century Modern style. Sometimes referred to as a "California Modern".

Craftsman

Identify this style by looking for rectangular and triangular shapes which characterize this no-nonsense design, built using natural local woods. These homes highlight simple hand-crafted wood construction. The front porch may have a separate, smaller roof and columns which echo the house. Nature-inspired exteriors reflect their surroundings with moss green, rusty red, and brown/tan colors. The front door will have glass near the top, and double-hung multi-tiered windows adorn the exterior. Pride of craftsmanship shines through, hence the name. Popular during the arts and crafts movement

Danish Provincial

This style is identified by the half-timber construction technique called bindingsværk, which uses brick and timber, or stucco and timber. The timber is arranged in an angle design. The thatched-roof look is common, as Scandinavian settlers brought their Danish designs straight from Denmark. Look around, the property may have an adjacent Danish windmill. And look up! You may see a stork weather vane sitting above the entrance, which the Danish believe will bring good luck to their family. Think: Solvang.

Federal

Look for a half-circle fanlight window over the door, symmetrical 2-story homes with tall doors and long, tall windows in a row. Greek columns welcome visitors to the small, formal front stoop (no porch) with double-hung sash windows, Palladian windows, and flat or low-pitched roofs. Interiors often boast circular, hexagon, and oval rooms with high ceilings. This formal, upscale style was popular from 1780 to 1850. Think: the White House and the Oval Room.

Foursquare

Popular in the Midwest, these homes are a staple style in Wisconsin, Minnesota, Indiana, Ohio, Michigan, and Illinois. Named "Foursquare" because the floor plan is 4 rooms per floor, boasting a square boxy shape with a wide front porch, these homes are often 2 stories with an attic dormer and a basement. The exterior has wood siding or shingles and is recognized by its square columns. This humble and basic floor plan is also known as "Prairie Box" and "American Foursquare".

French Country

This style reflects the French rural lifestyle, with designs ranging from modest farm houses to extravagant chateaus. These homes have a cottagey-feel and exude charm and character. They can be identified by the stone exterior, curved arches, wood-beam ceilings, and stone floors, and a thatched-roof look hipped roof. Colors are soft and blend in with the countryside. Think: Thomas Kinkade "light" paintings.

Georgian

Classic symmetry reigns supreme in this style inspired by the Renaissance movement. Outside, look for tall slender Greek-style columns adorning the front entrance, a hipped roof, and double-hung windows with shutters. Inside, key features are its graceful ornate detailed trim, a fireplace, and transom windows. Conservative colors are white, ivory, sand, light blue, or light gray. This is one of the earliest styles of architecture for homes built in New England between 1700 to1850. It bears a strong resemblance to the Federal style.

Gothic

Exterior features include: Steep tiered roof, arched or peaked/pointed windows and doorways, front door with a transom window above, diamond shaped window panes, and a small step-up front porch. Stone exterior walls are dark or tan/rock colored and feature stained glass windows. This Medieval style has an asymmetrical floor plan; look for ornate detailed trim, and crafted finials. Long-ago churches made this style popular, enhancing it by adding gorgeous stained windows and steeples. Popular in the 1840's to the 1890's, this style developed from America's Romantic Era. Think: dark haunted house.

Italianate

This formal European style is based on Italian design, framed by its signature Italian decorative double columns. It often has a square "cubed" tower with a cupola on top, or a campanile (bell tower). It boasts a paneled front door, often a double door, below the "tower" and a round transom window above the front door. Narrow, tall window panes extend from floor to ceiling and highlight the wrap-around porch. Unique characteristics are: tall, low-pitched roof, and crafted detailed brackets. Colors of this 2 or 3 story house with shutters and trim are usually white, green, or pinkish tan.

Log Cabin

This style is built with round tree logs, usually unpainted but logs may be enhanced to bring out and protect the natural wood look. This rustic, down-to-earth design is constructed using natural materials. It has a simple design with a pitched roof and a fireplace/chimney, set on a hill or a natural forest surrounding. This style is usually plain and functional and unpretentious; but fancy large variations can be found hidden away near upscale ski slopes. It's a popular style in mountainous regions of the west, particularly California, Montana, and Colorado, where these homes are used primarily as vacation cabins and snow/ski retreats. Think: lumber jack home.

Mediterranean

This popular California style is a combination of Spanish, Italian, and Greek influences, but with modern updates. It is a single or tiered-story design with a shallow sloping roof, arched windows and doorways, red tile roof, and an optional round tower room. Its wide, asymmetrical design is flanked by palm trees, tropical plants, and Mediterranean low-maintenance landscape. Inside, expect to find earthy natural materials, such as clay tiles, terracotta, and rustic wooden beams. This style is recently very popular in California, Nevada, and Florida. Tuscan style is a variation.

Mid-Century Modern

This style is identified by its clean lines, large airy spaces, and wide-open floor plans. Based on Scandinavian style designs, it has complete walls made of glass which create a "disappearing wall" effect that brings the outdoors inside and allows light to flood in. The entire building appears to be comprised of bold squares and geometric shapes. Its asymmetrical exterior design and minimalist features are a sharp contrast to natural surroundings. Colors are often simply black and white, with smoked gray windows and perhaps some unexpected punches of bright color. Think: Swanky Hollywood houses that look like museums. Also known as Art Deco or Moderne.

Mission

Developed from Spanish settlers, this is the classic Spanish style adapted to California's unique climate with its arched windows, doors, and doorways, red clay tile roof, minimal eaves with wood rafters peeking out, white stucco walls, 3 round pegs in the wall above the windows, and an optional square tower for the church bell. Interior courtyards are common, as are tile floors, open-beam ceilings, and black wrought iron work. This asymmetrical style was popular from 1890 to 1940 in the southwest, particularly Southern California, and it's unique to the southwest region. Think: the historic California Missions.

Overwater Hut

Specially designed for tropical locales, this simple bungalow-style home sits IN shallow water! It features a thatched roof harvested from local materials and piers to elevate it above the tide, with a wooden dock or stairway for access. A few amazing homes display glass bottom floors so residents can view the fish swimming. Desirable for resort vacation homes in tropical locations around the world, it's gaining popularity among the Gulf Coast regions, especially the Florida Cays. Think: Bora Bora island resort

Plantation

This boxy rectangle shaped 2-story house has a wide wrap-around front porch with tall white pillars and formal, stately designs. The gable roof has a medium pitch, and the balcony may wrap around the home. Long, tall French doors and windows bring light into this timeless, classic style. The symmetrical design is similar to Federal or Greek style. Also known as Southern Plantation from the antebellum south, this house design was popular in the South during the 1800's. Think: "Gone with the Wind" era.

Prairie

Identify this humble, earthy style architecture popularized by Frank Lloyd Wright with its single story, low roof line, broad eave overhang, and blocks of casement windows. This style takes advantage of natural light, often using stained glass patterns on the windows. The front door features glass in the top portion and a key characteristic is its asymmetric design, which makes the straight horizontal lines stand out. The interior is functional rather than fancy, boasting open spaces and very few doors in this utilitarian floor plan. Colors reflect browns, tans, and earth tones.

Pueblo

Built with adobe mud, this home was inspired by Pueblo/Native American mud homes in the desert. It's characterized by a flat roof, stucco/mud-look exterior walls with rounded edges, thick round roof beams, and a parapet wall (which peaks above the roof line). The arched doorway entrance (portico) is a nod to the Spanish and Mission styles, and this 1-story house blends in with its desert surroundings. This southwest style was popular in New Mexico and Arizona, particularly from 1912 to 1940. Also known as Santa Fe or Adobe.

Ranch

This popular architectural style in California is a single level house with low, long roof lines, stucco exterior, composition shingle roof, and an attached garage. Inside, the home has a simplistic floor plan, large wide casement windows, sliding glass doors to the backyard, wall-to-wall carpet, and vinyl flooring in the kitchen and bathroom. Its plain design is decorated with white, brown, or light pastel colors. Home builders began mass-producing ranch-style tract homes in the 1960's. Today, it is still the most popular style of house in California and ideally suited for rural country living. Farmhouse style is closely related.

Saltbox

This wood-frame style can be identified by its rectangle shaped house, 2 rooms deep and 2 stories high. It can be recognized by its long lop-sided roof, flat front, and chimney centrally placed. With symmetrical sides and noted for its elongated roof that slopes down the back, this classic eastern style is the basis for many other architectural styles, including Cape Cod, Federal, Georgian, and Plantation. It was most popular from 1800 to the 1920's.

Spanish

With designs very similar to the Mission style, this single-story home has an open courtyard, stucco exterior, red clay tile roof, black wrought iron detailing on windows and doors, blank white walls, and curved arches. The front door is a massive wooden oak door with hard-carved detailing, iron grille, and nail heads. Other exterior colors include off-white, pastel shades of pink, salmon, orange, or yellow. Inside, interior colors reflect a brightly colored heritage of sage green, teal blue, and sunset yellow, orange, and reds. It's similar to the Mission style and Early California style. Also known as Spanish Colonial or Spanish Revival.

Swiss Chalet

Based on Danish design, this stylish home is typically found in mountainous regions and forests, often used as a vacation home in resort destinations such as Lake Tahoe and Yosemite. It may be built on a hill side amongst trees. Its characteristics include 2½ stories of a rectangular shape with a low pitched roof and decorative brackets under wide eaves. The exterior may be a combination of wood, stucco, brick, or stone. It has a high pointed roof and the exterior wood is arranged in a traditional decorative Scandinavian-style pattern. An exterior staircase leads up to the 2nd story living areas upstairs. Colorful, blooming flowers are planted under the windows and in window boxes. And don't be surprised to find a Swiss flag hanging in the front!

Tudor

Based on the English Cottage design, this 1-story house has high, pointed roof lines that contain several peaks, ornate wood millwork, diamond-pattern window panes, asymmetric design, and an attic with a dormer. Unique features include half-timbering with brickwork, tall windows, high fireplace/chimneys, and thatched roofs. This rustic, simple style was popular from 1910 to 1940. Compare to French Country style.

Victorian

Charm and character exudes from these classic stylish homes. Each one is a unique, hand-built house with no standard door or window sizes. Highlights include tall elevations, intricate details, and superb craftsmanship such as wood scalloped shingles or narrow horizontal slats. The design is asymmetric, usually 2 to 3 story, with a small lot "footprint". Key characteristics are: high, peaked roof, wide front porch, long tall windows, steep staircases, contrasting pastel tones, and hand-carved "gingerbread" motif. Interior features include ceiling medallions, chair rails, crown molding, and plaster walls. Designs can range from the humble, plain, 1-story to the extravagantly detailed 3-story with a tower. Victorian sub-styles include: Queen Ann, Richardsonian, Folk, and Stick Style. Think: the "Painted Ladies" in downtown San Francisco.

NOTE: Refer to our "GREEN" chapter for more architectural styles such as EarthShip, Geodesic Dome, Round House, and Earth Bermed.

Conclusion

How many different home styles are in your neighborhood? Learn to identify house architecture in your farm area when you drive around. Not sure of the style? Snap a photo and verify it online to see if you identified the house correctly. Speak intelligently when advising your clients, and you'll quickly become the sought-after neighborhood resource.

Now you're a home architecture pro and you can speak intelligently when advising your clients. And at the next sunset soiree, impress your friends with your newfound knowledge of house architecture. You'll be the life of the party!

2. Historic & Vintage Features

View sample illustrations on our pinterest board:

http://www.pinterest.com/realtyproadvisr/historic-vintage-homes

Historic homes, often built over a century ago, capture the essence of a significant time period in history, or were inhabited by famous people. Vintage homes are revered for their character, charm, and distinct style. Buyers seeking to purchase historic homes are searching for buildings that appeal to their architectural, scenic, cultural, or visual flair.

Historically designated buildings, whether occupied or vacant, are carefully preserved and thoughtfully restored to the original carpentry. Architectural styles include Georgian, Colonial, Victorian, Early California, Romanesque Revival, Old World Spanish, Federal, and Greek Revival. Following are some of the features to look for in historic homes.

Exterior

Historic homes are visually attractive because of their unique hand-crafted exteriors. Here are a few things to look for:

Brackets

Metal or wooden supports which appear to support the roof. Often carved with ornate scrollwork or characteristic designs.

Bulkhead

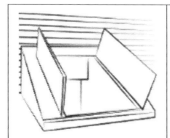

A set of thick, tornado-proof doors that open into a cellar underneath the home.

Buttress

Triangular wall supports made of brick or stone, unique to Gothic styles architecture.

Clapboard

Exterior siding on a building, comprised of narrow slats of wood which overlap downwards. Weatherboard is similar to clapboard, but the boards are wider.

Coping

Wall caps that serve as weather protection, but also designed to enhance the home's architectural style.

Finial

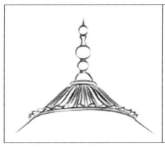

A tall spike, common to the Gothic period, at the top of a roof, metal gate bars, cupola, or spire.

Frieze

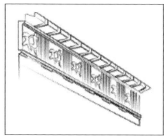	The panel directly below a cornice, and resting on the columns or piers. It is often decorated with unique medallions or dentil designs.

Pendant

	A decorative metal or wood piece that hangs under a porch, ornamental bracket, or cornice.

Portico

	A small front porch stoop with support columns and a small pitched roof.

Quoins

	Stone, wood, or brick rectangles which overlap the corners of a wall to enhance the style.

Roof

Vintage homes may be recognized by their unique roof styles and vintage era towers:

Cornice

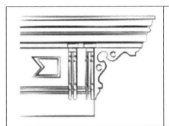

Edge of the roof, finished with ornaments, or decorated with medallions, brackets, or dentil features.

Cresting

Decorative wrought iron trim installed at the top or border of a roof. Popular in Mansard architecture.

Dormer

A roof-opening window in the attic. Styles include Gabled dormer, Shed dormer, and Eyelid dormer.

Parapet

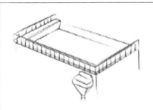

A roof or porch top constructed of brick or stone walls, with some areas that rise above the flat areas. **Battlements** are the sections that are lower than the tall sections. A **Crenalated parapet** means that it has regular breaks.

Pediment

Small porch slanted roof facing towards the front of a building, and popular in Classical Revival architecture.

Pent Roof

	On a multi-story building, a slanted roof piece attached to the wall, above the lower story, often wrapping around the entire building.

Tower

	A round, tall room with a pointed top. A **Tourelle** is a smaller tower with corbel trim. A **Turret** is a corner tower. A **Cupola** is a square or octagon shaped tower at the top of a roof, often with a decorative weathervane on top.

Columns

Historic homes often feature columns on porches, exteriors, and interiors.

Columns

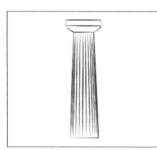	Round support pillars, with classic architectural detailing.

Pedestal

	Refers to the bottom portion of a column, often a thick base which is slightly decorative, and matches the architectural style of the capital at the top.

Fluting

	The decorative finish with vertical grooves that adds texture and style.

Capitals

	Refer to the decorative caps at the top of the columns. Capital architectural styles include Roman, Green, Corinthian, and Ionic.

Pilasters

	Narrow columns attached to a wall, which appear to be free-standing columns.

Pillars

	Plain columns, either stand-alone, or in a patterned row.

Windows

Historic homes are recognized for their unique window styles. Below are a few types of windows that distinguish historic and vintage homes.

Arched

	Rounded or segmental arches that highlight a window or a door.

Fanlight

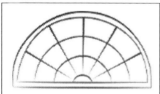	A half-circle shaped non-opening window placed above a doorway. Decorative styles reflect the time period of the construction.

Oriel

	A 3-sided bay window with decorative support brackets.

Palladian

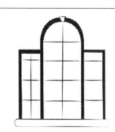	Tall arched window with 2 side windows, popular in Colonial and Georgian homes.

Tracery

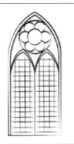	Curved window with a pointed arch at the top. Decorative metal designs highlight this Gothic style architecture.

Transom

	A non-opening window placed above a door to bring light in the room, often multi-paned for visual effect.

Interior

Once you get inside the home, you and your buyers can admire the many unique characteristics of a historic home:

Chair Rail

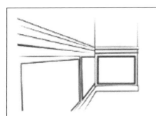	Wooden strip of molding that is tacked horizontally mid-way up the side of a wall. The purpose is to protect the wall from chair backs and to give a decorative, uniform finish.

Corbel

	A stone or wooden bracket / dentil, placed on a wall and having the appearance of holding up a roof, mantle, or shelf.

Molding

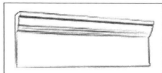	Wooden strip or panel placed flush against the top of a wall and ceiling. Also seen on windows, walls, doors, and columns as a decorative feature known as a crown.

Niche

	Small cubby hole inset in a wall, either square or arched, to display art.

Tudor Arch

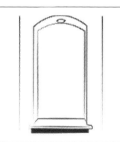	Arched doorway or window that comes to a point at the top. Common in Tudor Revival style architecture, also known as a 4-centered arch.

Wainscot

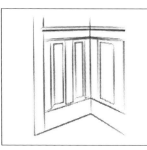	Wooden panel on the lower half of a wall, often with a chair rail above. Panels may have trim or decorative patterns.

Conclusion

When you view a historic home, take a careful look at its unique features. Perhaps the house is listed on the "National Register of Historic Places", which is quite an honor. Even if only designated as a local landmark, the property contributes aesthetic beauty to its local neighborhood.

With this handy guide, you will now be able to advise your clients who are seeking vintage charm and old-world character. One day you may even choose to specialize in historic homes!

3. Gourmet Kitchens

View sample illustrations on our pinterest board:

http://www.pinterest.com/realtyproadvisr/gourmet-kitchens

The kitchen is the heart of the home; the place where families gather, hosts entertain, and generations pass on traditions. And yeah... we cook food there too! Kitchens are often the most decisive room for home-shopping buyers — especially meticulous wives and aspiring chefs.

Layouts

A comfortable kitchen layout sets the atmosphere and determines the workflow. A lavish kitchen is uniquely custom designed with a well-appointed layout.

U-Shaped Kitchen

 Spacious U-shaped layouts offer more cooking room, counter space, and often a breakfast bar.

Circular Kitchen

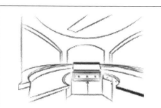 Circular kitchens offer the convenience of counters and appliances in close proximity without being interrupted by doorways.

L-shaped Kitchen

 L-shaped counters are often combined with an island or peninsula.

Galley Kitchen

 | Traditional galley layouts are being scrapped in favor of bright, open kitchens that allow cooks and guests to chat while preparing meals and entertaining.

Cabinets

Decadent cabinets define a high caliber kitchen. Kitchen designers look for sophisticated knobs and pulls with complementary matching hinges, and detailed features such as finishing touches of crown molding above cabinets. Small details make a big difference in a high end kitchen.

Upscale cabinet finishes range from solid wood (favorites are cherry, maple, oak, and pine) to laminate and lacquered cabinets. Innovative cabinets include slide-out shelves, spice rack pullouts, and self-closing drawers. A "drawer in drawer" is a mini drawer, similar to a drawer insert, that's tucked inside of a large drawer. It's perfect for silverware, utensils, or linens for special occasions.

Turn an unused corner into an accessible shelf with a ¾ turntable that spins out. Even better, a "Magic Corner" allows full utilization of the dead space in a corner cabinet, by swinging out the front shelf and pulling the corner shelf forward.

Cabinets are typically constructed of wood, but can also be crafted from melamine and composite products. Cabinets were formerly known as cupboards.

	Slide-out shelves
	Spice rack pullouts
	Self-closing drawers

	Drawer in drawer

Counters

The shiny polished look of granite is being edged out by honed granite which sports a matte finish. Today's trendy glass tile and recycled crafted glass surfaces are quickly replacing the standard ceramic tile counter tops. Other recycled materials include concrete, paper, plastic, and other composites.

Laminate solid surfaces, such as Formica®, mimic the high end look of travertine at a fraction of the cost. The simple contemporary styling of Staron (acrylic) and Radianz (quartz) can lend a luxurious personal touch. Other custom solid surfaces include Avonite, Swanstone, and Corian®.

A butcher block counter hand-crafted from solid wood doubles as a cutting board and offers a warm, welcoming flair. A custom designed kitchen may feature solid travertine, carrara marble, or exotic stone counters. Modern selections include copper, soapstone, or metal such as copper and stainless steel.

Look for elegantly contrasting backsplashes with horizontal glass tiles, copper/tin/bronze square tiles, or ivory subway tiles. More fashionable kitchens include old world hand-painted wall mosaics and embossed textured concrete that has been stained and stamped for a modernistic appeal.

Counter Layouts

Island

	An island is a stand-alone fixture in the middle of the kitchen. It usually has cabinets underneath and is topped with a counter that compliments the other counters. It may contain a stove, sink, or dishwasher. A popular layout is an island counter with bar stools.

L-shaped Counter

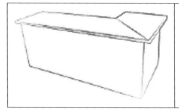	An L-shaped counter wraps around 2 adjacent walls to give a lot of counter space for prepping and serving food.

Breakfast Bar

A breakfast bar has a counter that projects out above the cabinets, allowing leg room for people to sit in chairs. It may be at table-height, or higher at bar-height.

Kitchen Peninsula

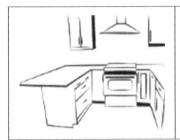

A kitchen peninsula is a set of cabinets with a counter attached to the rest of the kitchen counters, but it is not butted up against a wall. The peninsula may be used as a breakfast bar.

Large Appliances

Major appliances, built-in and color-matched, add tremendous value to a kitchen. Eco-conscious "green" products promote energy sustainability while saving money on power bills, and Energy Star® qualified appliances can earn tax rebates.

Look for slate (a matte silver finish) to replace stainless steel as the hottest trend. White ice and black ice colors help major appliances can break out of the black/white tradition. Custom colors bring dynamic pops of red, yellow, or teal blue. For a refined finish, almond or ivory colors coordinate with the earth-tone palette perfectly.

Refrigerators

Double-door refrigerators just don't make the cut any longer. Discriminating homeowners are spending extra for mega capacity French door refrigerators (side-by-side top with bottom freezer drawer) to accommodate their family's food storage needs. And integrated with cabinet panels covering the doors, large fridges blend seamlessly into the background. With refrigerators, interior space is measured in terms of cubic feet.

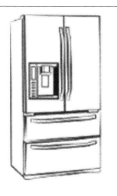

Top-of-the-line fridges include convenient features like:

- Ice maker and ice crusher
- Tall water / ice dispenser area
- Multi-tiered shelves
- Door-in-door easy access to drinks & snacks
- Blast chiller
- Mini-drawers that flex
- Vegetable settings to de-humidify and keep veggies fresh
- Compact refrigerated drawers at kid-height.

Commercial-Grade Refrigerators

For serious home chefs, a commercial grade refrigerator is the perfect solution. These robust appliances installed in luxury homes are wider, taller, and much heavier. The highly renowned Sub-Zero brand features water filtration, air purification, and dual-refrigeration technology behind a control console.

Fridge Drawers

Family friendly fridge drawers are perfect for children's juices and snacks.

Dishwashers

When it comes to dishwashers, think outside the traditional built-in under cabinet dishwasher. Save space with contemporary options such as:

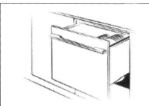

Drawer dishwashers (AKA dishdrawers)

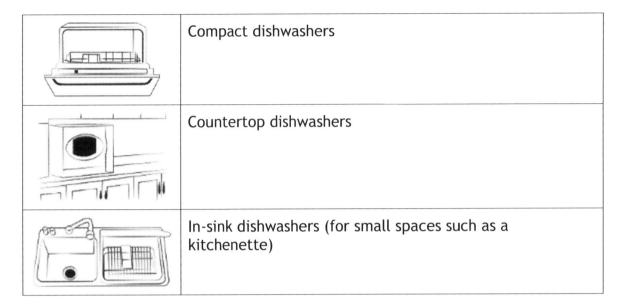	Compact dishwashers
	Countertop dishwashers
	In-sink dishwashers (for small spaces such as a kitchenette)

Stove / Oven / Range

What is the difference between a stove, oven, and range? A stove is a cooktop that houses the burners for cooking with pots and pans. An oven bakes and roasts food inside, and often has a broiler underneath. A range is the kitchen appliance that combines both the oven and the stove into one unit.

On a stove, do the burners offer quick-boil and low-simmer settings? Does it have pilotless ignition? Do the rings lift off for authentic wok cooking? Other great features that chefs crave:

- Griddle Top
- Char-broiler
- French Plate
- Hot Top
- Graduated French Top

Induction electric cooktops with a smooth glass surface provide nearly instant heat for a metal pan, yet are safe to the touch for cooks. Features include multiple settings and count-down timers. Induction heating is an impressive tech advancement beyond the standard ceramic electric stovetop.

	**Stove.** Every chef's dream kitchen certainly includes a gourmet stove cooktop. Wolf commercial cooktops with 6 gas open burners are regarded as the standard for home chefs preparing high quality meals

	**Oven.** The cooking can be powered by fuel (gas or propane) or by electricity. However, modern gas stoves also need electricity to power all the fancy features, such as the clock, alarm, lights, and programming.
	**Range.** In a gourmet kitchen, don't expect to see slide-in or freestanding ranges. Instead, double ovens, convection ovens, and custom installation ovens are the standard of luxury. Look for features such as a self-cleaning oven, an adjustable broiler, a warming drawer, and child lock-out safety feature.
	**Commercial-Grade Range.** For home chefs who enjoy cooking and baking restaurant quality meals, the Wolf brand is respected as first class and often seen in luxury homes. With 2 ovens side by side, custom-designed cooktops feature an infrared griddle, infrared charbroiler, and/or French cooktop. Sturdy construction quality is highlighted by red signature knobs.

Convection ovens are desirable for their quick and even cooking because it has a high-speed fan that circulates heated air as the food is being cooked. Regarded as a home cook's favorite oven, often a custom kitchen will include a convection oven for roasting.

The new look includes retro appliances too! Antique ranges such Gold medal, Glenwood, and Brookline are lovingly restored to highlight their heirloom value. These one-of-a-kind vintage ranges bring unique character and charm into a kitchen, highlighting the home owner's individuality.

Hood Vents

Hood vents serve the function of removing the smoke from the stove, but can also bring beautiful aesthetic design into a kitchen. They come in every style to suit the custom designed home, including modern styles such as:

	Wall mount

	Chimney hood
	Island mount
	Under cabinet
	Pro hoods
	Downdraft hoods. Island stoves may include a fan vent that pops up from behind, eliminating the need for a hood vent above.
	Power packs
	Built-in / Insert blower
	Mantel style

 A micro-hood, a microwave that doubles as a stove hood vent, helps keep the counter looking spacious and clutter-free.

Other Appliances

Elaborate homes boast a built-in trash compactor, and most likely a recycle bin too. A built-in deep fryer is another great appliance on every chef's wish list. Gourmet smoking ovens are at the top of the list too. And don't forget that wood-fired pizza oven for the folks who really enjoy entertaining.

Sinks

Don't hide that gorgeous sink; it can be the star of the kitchen! A tasteful sink should be functional as well as beautiful. Cooks want a sink with 2 or 3 basins, preferably one shallow basin for washing veggies. One basin is expected to be equipped with a garbage disposal. An elaborate kitchen will boast 2 sinks: the main sink in the counter against a wall, and a prep sink in the island counter. Expect to see a third sink — a bar sink — in homes built for entertainment and parties.

Sink Materials

Sinks can be made from materials such as:

- **Stainless steel** - very durable and most popular
- **Porcelain** – typically constructed from vitreous white china
- **Acrylic** – scratch resistant, and can be painted in customized colors
- **Cast iron** – old fashioned and least expensive material, can show rust and signs of wear. May be coated with enamel to help preserve from wear and tear.
- **Granite** – expensive yet easy to maintain; look for various grade of granite
- **Copper** – will not corrode or rust, and if not polished, develops a green patina
- **Stone** – beautiful custom carved designed; elegant but expensive
- **Fireclay** – fine quality construction is hardy and heavy

Sink Styles

Common styles include the traditional top-mount and the nouveau under-mount. Seen more frequently in upscale designs, the farmhouse / apron-front sink style adds a punch of style to the kitchen ambiance.

Topmount Sink

	Installed above the counter, and has a rim which provides a nice trimmed finish. It's also known as a "drop-in" sink.

Undermount Sink

	Installed under the counter, so it needs to be supported underneath. Since there is no rim, it has a sleek modern look.

Farmhouse / Apron-Front Sink

	Large, deep, single basins that project out from the counter and cabinets. They are more difficult to install because the counter must be designed specifically around the sink.

Garbage Disposal

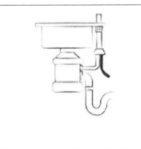	Every sink needs a garbage disposal, also known as a food waste disposal. Contrary to popular belief, a disposal does not work with a blade at the bottom like a blender. Instead, it propels the food at a high rate to the sides, where the food particles are shredded. Disposals are rated in terms of horsepower; the more horsepower, the stronger its operating ability and the higher the quality.

Faucets & Hardware

A well-chosen faucet can complement the sink and tie in the entire kitchen design. Kitchens with multiple sinks will have matching faucets. Faucets may have a single handle or two separate handles, one lever for each hot and cold. Single handles are easier to operate, with the handle on either the back or the side of the spout.

Faucet Styles

Faucet styles include the following:

Low Arc Spout

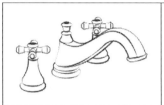

| | The spout projects horizontally in this classic design. |

High Arc Spout

| | The spout curves up and down graciously in an upside-down "U" shape. |

Mid Arc Spout

| | The spout curves upwards gently. |

Pull-Out Spray Nozzle

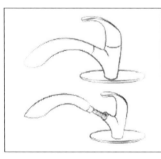

| | This traditional style allows you to use the faucet regularly, or you can pull down the nozzle. Great for washing vegetables or cleaning dishes without having a separate spray nozzle on the side of the sink. |

Pull Down Spray Nozzle

| | This high arc spout also has a nozzle that can be pulled (down, not out). |

Wall Mount Faucet

	Installed directly into the wall, this style achieves a minimalist look and leaves less clutter on the counter.

Bridge Faucet

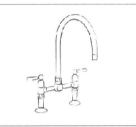	Chic and stylish, this design sports 2 handles and a U-shaped spout that swings around.

Faucet Accessories

As if those are not enough choices, here are more ways to add interesting and exotic features to the sink. Some of our favorites include:

Touch-On

	The on/off switch is built into the spout, so you can simply touch it and the faucet turns on.

LED Neon Tap

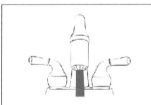	A unique way to bring a colorful burst into the kitchen, a red, blue, or green neon light comes on when water is flowing, making the water glow colorfully.

Pot Filler

	Authentic Italian kitchens are often equipped with a wall-mount faucet above the stove to fill deep pasta pots conveniently. May be installed on the deck / counter or directly into the wall.

Additional Nozzles & Valves

Sinks may include several types of gadgets: side spray nozzles, dishwasher aerator valves, beverage faucets, and soap dispensers.

Side Spray Nozzle

	Individual spray nozzle that is installed separately from the spout. The hose pulls out with adjustable nozzle options: spray, stream, and pause.

Dishwasher Aerator Valve

	A metal valve installed near the sink, above the dishwasher, to allow air ventilation from the dishwasher while running.

Beverage Faucet

	Specific faucet on the side of the sink that is connected to a purified drinking water source.

Faucet Materials

Traditional faucets are made from stainless steel, which is shiny when polished. More modern finishes seen in gourmet kitchens include: oil-rubbed bronze, antique gold, brushed nickel, brass, pewter, and mixed metals.

Flooring

Kitchen flooring sets the tone for a well-finished look. Elegant kitchens include durable, long-lasting easy-to-clean sleek flooring. Because the kitchen is the "heart of the home" the flooring needs to withstand traffic 3 times per day. Of course, the flooring needs to be water-resistant, since a kitchen will have water and other liquid spills.

Flooring Materials

Kitchen flooring types include the following materials:

- **Bamboo** – it looks like wood, but this high-density flooring is made from giant bamboo plants (which are a type of grass, not a tree). Valued for its cozy look and "green" sustainability.
- **Ceramic tile** – large square tiles, often 12" x 12", installed on a prepped surface with grout in between each tile. Grout colors can match or complement the tile. Design options include a retro black & white checkerboard design, a diamond pattern, or intricate custom patterns.
- **Concrete** – for a modern no-frills industrial look, concrete designs are endless because the floor can be stamped and stained in various colors, and designs can be etched with acid.
- **Cork** – natural cork harvested from trees, this flooring is more comfortable for standing and provides a layer of insulation.
- **Hardwood planks** – solid wood installed in thin or thick strips in a vertical or horizontal pattern, including oak, pine, or maple. Higher quality hardwood can be expensive, but lasts forever. Recycled timber floors provide an environmentally friendly option.
- **Laminate / engineered wood** – typically a wood-look which is less expensive than real hardwood, the planks "float" because they are hooked into each other instead of being nailed to the floor.
- **Linoleum** – the classic 50's kitchen flooring. Different from vinyl because it's manufactured using natural materials such as linseed oil, linoleum is coming back into vogue because of its "green" reputation.
- **Stone** – natural authentic granite, slate, limestone, and travertine are popular stone types because each stone has a unique variation.
- **Porcelain tile** – all the rage lately, these fabulous glazed wood look-alike tiles are installed with long, narrow strips of solid and sturdy ceramic.
- **Vinyl** – synthetic material sheets are rolled out to cover the entire floor at once. Once viewed as cheap, new modern vinyl looks amazingly like real wood, tile, or stone.

Lighting

Glowing lights lend ambiance for a lavish kitchen. The right lighting can set the warm mood for welcoming family and friends.

Gone are the days of drop-down ceilings with fluorescent light tubes. Today's gourmet kitchen may include false soffits for old-world character and charm, pendant lights over the island or breakfast bar, and a custom vintage crystal chandelier.

Under cabinet lights radiate across the counters and provide task lighting for preparing large meals. Recessed lighting, also known as "pot lights" shines directly over specific areas. Uplighting is a great way to flood the kitchen with simulated daylight.

Accessories & Miscellaneous

How about a kitchen that pops with really cool gadgets? Try a magnetic spice rack, a pop-up appliance, and a pull-out pet feeding area. To send your kitchen over the top, borrow ideas from commercial kitchens: a wine cooler with separate temperature controls for white and red wines, and food warmer drawers that hide in the cabinet.

Pop-up Appliances

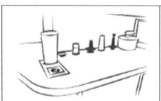 Appliances that pop up from the counter top are convenient for cooking. Blenders and mixers are popular small appliances.

Wine Cooler

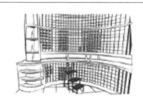 Wine storage areas are often located in a basement or cellar, because wine bottles are best stored and served at a cooler temperature. In an upscale home, look for temperature-controlled climates with an automatic thermostat to protect the integrity of the wines.

Food Warmer

 Food warmers, a concept borrowed from commercial kitchens, keeps hot foods warm (without burning) while preparing a meal. Great for large gatherings.

Pantry

Every kitchen needs a pantry, but a deluxe kitchen needs a luxurious touch. Look for variations on the standard shelving, including a slide-out tall pantry, a walk-in pantry room, floor-to-ceiling spinning lazy susans, hinged shelving that swings out, built-in vegetable bins, or a corner pantry. Doors can convey a polished look to the pantry, including translucent panels, stained glass, or frosted glass door. A kid-friendly pantry door can be a chalkboard for spelling fun or a place for parents to write a shopping list.

Spinning Lazy Susan

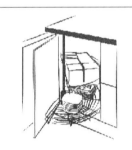

A lazy susan is a round circle-shaped platform on a rolling base that spins around for convenience in retrieving items. Popularly used in a cabinet for vitamin storage, the concept was adapted to cabinet shelving. They can be installed in a corner or other hard-to-reach places, which allows easy access to otherwise "dead" spaces in the back of the cabinet.

Butler's Pantry

A home built for entertaining will certainly have a butler's pantry suitable as a staging area for parties. The butler's pantry is used to store fine china, wine glasses, and elegant serve-ware. Caterers and cooks use it as a serving prep area.

Wine Cellar

Designer wine racks define the discerning home owner. Hanging wine racks on the wall, or above an island, provide sliding storage underneath for stemware. Look for wine racks built into the side of an island, or a climate-controlled wine cellar. Besides the usual wooden racks, wine enthusiasts can incorporate flair into their kitchens with unique metal bottle holders.

Pull-Out Waste Basket

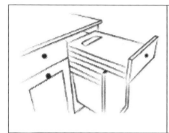

Eco-conscious home buyers demand green features, such as pull-out waste baskets to separate the recyclable materials with ease. Other environmentally friendly kitchen conveniences include an herb-growing planter box, built-in soap and lotion dispensers, and cool air storage bins for vegetables.

Appliance Garage

An appliance garage is a great way of keeping counters clean and neat by hiding small appliances. Find an appliance garage hiding behind a wooden sliding door that matches the counters, or a shiny metal roll-up door. They are most efficient when located near electric outlets for convenient appliance use.

Conclusion

We hope you enjoyed the gourmet kitchen tour. With so many different features, there is much to learn, isn't there! Are you ready to find out which listings have which amenities? Simply bring this guide along next time you preview a house. Then, when viewing homes with your clients, you'll be ready to explain all those interesting features. And you'll truly be respected as the real estate specialist!

4. Luxury Bathrooms

View sample illustrations on our pinterest board:

http://www.pinterest.com/realtyproadvisr/luxury-bathrooms

No dream home is complete without a luxury bathroom! Today's trendy homeowners are adding extravagant spa-like bathrooms to enjoy a relaxing oasis and calming sanctuary. But you don't need an opulent million-dollar home to have a bathroom as posh as an affluent hotel spa.

Home owners can improve their house with sumptuous features and ambient glowing lighting without splurging their entire budget. All they need is a bit of inspiration to create a rich, romantic look. Follow our glossary guide below to discover some of the unique features you may find in a deluxe bathroom.

Bathroom Types

Luxury bathrooms are built in a variety of configurations. A popular trend is home bathrooms that mimic high-end lavish resorts, granting the homeowner an oasis to escape from the everyday hustle and bustle and relax comfortably.

Ensuite Bathroom

	A bathroom that is adjacent to, and accessed only from, a bedroom. Usually applies to a master bathroom attached to the master bedroom. Pronounced "ON-sweet". Can also be spelled as 2 words, "en suite".

Jack & Jill Bathroom

	A bathroom sandwiched in between 2 bedrooms, with access from each bedroom. It has 2 doors, from each bedroom, and usually no door to a hallway or common area.

Powder Room

A half bathroom with only a sink and toilet. Often near the common areas, instead of the bedrooms, so that it's easily available for guests. In houses with 2 stories, the bottom level (living room, dining room, kitchen, etc.) often has a powder room for convenient access, so guests don't have to walk upstairs for the bathroom.

Bath Tubs

Bathtubs, commonly referred to as "tubs", are used for the traditional bathing method of immersing in water. Tubs today, however, are anything but traditional!

Freestanding Tub

This original style of bathtub is not built in or attached to a wall. If it also includes a shower head, it is surrounded by drapes hanging from suspended rods to keep the water intact. Can be crafted from porcelain or ceramic.

Clawfoot Tub

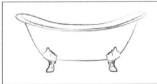

Clawfoot tub is an antique style in which the tub sits on 4 decorative metal legs.

Garden Tub

Large, luxurious bathtub made for soaking (no jets). Often situated under a window for maximum light and a garden view.

Jetted / Whirlpool Tub

Deep bathtub with hydrotherapy jets for warm water. May have an in-line heater. Jacuzzi is a common brand.

Corner Tub

Bathtub with a triangular shaped basin, usually large enough for 2 people. Can be drop-in installation or freestanding. Popular in the honeymoon suite or on Valentine's day when shaped as a heart.

Japanese Ofuro Soaking Tub

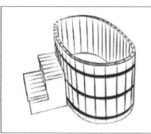

Deep, sunken hot tub with freshly poured water and no chemicals. Traditionally crafted from hinoki wood but modern versions can be made from other materials.

Showers

Stand-alone showers are seen in bathrooms with or without a stand-alone bathtub. Often they are combined with a tub by adding a shower head to the wall above the tub to have the effect of 2 features in 1 component.

Rain Shower Heads

The ultimate spa experience begins with an oversized, rain drop shower head, imitating the feeling of a gentle rain from overhead. Paired with body sprays, rain showers can turn a simple shower into a luxurious spa feeling.

Frameless Glass Panel

A shower made entirely of clear glass panels with no trim and very little hardware. The minimalist panels are often suspended from overhead tracks. This sleek, modern shower makes the bathroom appear open and spacious.

Roman Shower

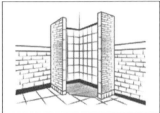

A large walk-in shower cavity with no door and no rim on the edge from the floor. Often created with bricks or stone to mimic the ancient styles. Great access for wheelchairs, walkers, or those with limited mobility.

Sauna / Steam Room

Swanky homes boast steam showers and saunas, lauded for health benefits. Steam showers feature high tech gadgets, while traditional saunas are often crafted from plain wood.

Steam Shower

An enclosed room similar to a shower, wherein steam generates a water vapor around the body. Built with tile, stone, wood, or other materials. Can be used by multiple people at once.

Aromatherapy Steam Shower

Essential oils infused into the steam (water vapor) for health benefits.

Sauna

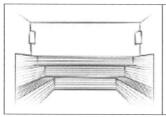

Wooden air-tight humid cabin filled with steam for health benefits. Believed to relieve stress and tension, rejuvenate the skin, help the body eliminate toxins, and stimulate blood circulation. Styles include either wet or dry saunas.

Vanity & Sink

A sink is much more than just a place to wash hands — it can add style and elegance to the bathroom. Combined with an eye-catching vanity, a bathroom can be a dazzling oasis for home owners.

Dual / Double Vanity

Counter with 2 sinks. Master bathrooms may be designed with a "his" and "hers" sink and vanity area.

Vessel Sink

Bowl or dish, often glass or ceramic, that sits on top of the counter. Becoming more popular in luxury homes.

Floating Countertop

Wall-mounted cabinet and sink are not resting on the floor and appear to be "floating". May have a towel storage area underneath.

Vintage Vanities

	Hand-crafted from an antique chest of drawers, an old cabinet, or a marble-top buffet, vintage furnishings are often custom made.

Toilet

Sometimes referred to as the "loo" or the "john", gone are the days of blah and boring ceramic toilets. These days, look for toilets with high tech features such as touchless lift seats and touchless flushing. Check out our "GREEN" homes section for additional toilet options, such as a dual flush toilet & composting toilet.

Bidet

	Toilet-like fixture used for rinsing or washing intimate body parts. Not yet very popular in the U.S., it's commonly used internationally as an alternative or addition to toilet paper. A full bath with a bidet may be referred to as a "5/4" bathroom. Pronounced "bi-DAY".

Touchless

	Touchless lift seat features uses a sensor to lift the seat with a wave of the hand. It draws raves from both husbands and wives alike; and who knows – it just may put an end to that age-old seat up/down dispute!
	Touchless flush goes down magically with a simple wave of the hand. Could prevent germ exposure on a dirty handle!

Windows & Window Treatments

Windows bring daylight into a small bathroom and enlarge a spacious one. Most importantly, windows provide ventilation and prevent mold build-up from the steam. They also help air out smelly odors. Windows can be decorative as well as functional.

Light with Privacy

Glass blocks, stained glass windows, and translucent windows provide privacy while letting in lots of daylight. Tempered glass is a safety must for low bathrooms windows.

Drapes & Curtains

Besides the usual blinds and shutters, consider designing the bathroom with sheer curtains that allow light or with drapes made of luxurious velvet or silk. Don't forget frilly embellishments such as tassels, beads, and fringe.

Lighting

Lights can either date a bathroom or enhance the modern design. Here's a few trendy options. Stay tuned...we'll show you more lighting options in the next chapter.

Pendant Lights

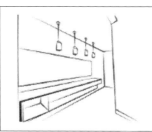

Enjoy lighting at the right level by installing ceiling pendant lights. Either in a track, or installed separately, they add a radiant glow. Look for mini-pendant halogen lights, star pendant designs, or drum-shade style lights.

Green Lighting

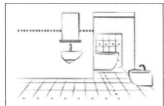

Skylights, halogen bulbs, and high tech recessed LED lights are bringing new "green" solutions that outshine the traditional fluorescent light fixtures. LED lights offer higher energy efficiency, due to their lower voltage compared to incandescent light bulbs.

ChromoTherapy

	Colored lights in the bathtub are believed to bring healing qualities and energy with light therapy. Enjoyed by holistic health seekers to soothe, invigorate, and empower.

Unique Solutions

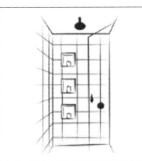	Homeowners opting for amazing lighting are choosing unexpected fixtures such as chandeliers, custom sconces, and candle niches with eye-catching candleholders.

Hardware & Accessories

Blissful bathrooms may include unique accessories such as a fish tank, fireplace, heated towel rack, surround sound music, and a flat screen TV mounted behind a one-way mirror. Look for hardware finishes such as oil-rubbed bronze, antique nickel, wrought iron, French gold, antique copper, and brushed chrome. Plush touches include teak mats and open shelving with plants, flowers, and jars.

Building Materials

Natural materials gaining in popularity amongst home renovators include reclaimed lumber, pebbles, bamboo, granite, teak, maple, chrome, and limestone. Variations of tile used for backsplashes and counters include tumbled beach glass tile, hand crafted glass tile, and marble tile. Expect to see rich touches of gilt and crystal woven into the design.

Flooring

Splendid new trends in flooring include natural stone floors, wood-textured porcelain tile floor, slip-resistant concrete, bamboo flooring, cork tiles. A heated tile floor (with radiant-heat coils) is certainly a luxurious touch for cold weather climates. But perhaps the most innovate feature is a tub set in a fiberglass pan filled with glossy black river rocks to exude an "outdoor" feeling.

Conclusion

When you snag that listing for the luxury home for sale, now you know what bathroom features to identify. Discover new tech gadgets like LED lighting, chromotherapy, and the TV hidden behind the mirror. Learn the lingo to identify all types of tubs, showers, and vanities so you can help buyers find their dream home!

5. Major Appliances

View sample illustrations on our pinterest board:

http://www.pinterest.com/realtyproadvisr/major-appliances

Appliances reveal a lot about a home. Buyers may gauge the likeability of a house based on the brand, style, and finish of the appliances. Yes we all know our buyers "Can always buy a nicer fridge after they move in." But they want to know what is in the house now. Don't let them down. Satisfy their thirst for knowledge by cluing them in on the latest major appliances.

Refrigerators

Double-door refrigerators just don't make the cut any longer. Discriminating homeowners are spending extra for mega capacity French door refrigerators (side-by-side top with bottom freezer drawer) to accommodate their family's food storage needs. And integrated with cabinet panels covering the doors, large fridges blend seamlessly into the background. With refrigerators, interior space is measured in terms of cubic feet.

Top-of-the-line fridges include convenient features such as:

	Ice maker and ice crusher
	Tall water / ice dispenser area
	Multi-tiered shelves

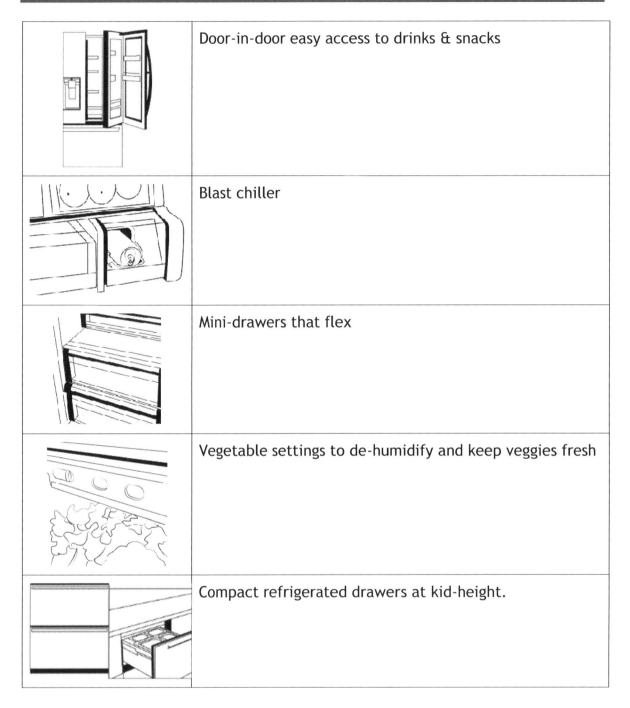

	Door-in-door easy access to drinks & snacks
	Blast chiller
	Mini-drawers that flex
	Vegetable settings to de-humidify and keep veggies fresh
	Compact refrigerated drawers at kid-height.

Dishwashers

When it comes to dishwashers, think outside the traditional built-in under cabinet dishwasher. Save space with contemporary options such as:

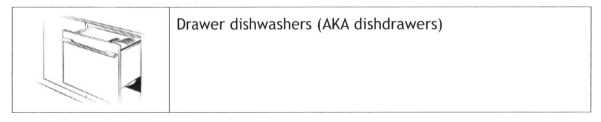

	Drawer dishwashers (AKA dishdrawers)

	Compact dishwashers
	Countertop dishwashers
	In-sink dishwashers (for small spaces such as a kitchenette)

Stove / Oven / Range

What is the difference between a stove, oven, and range? A stove is a cooktop that houses the burners for cooking with pots and pans. An oven bakes and roasts food inside, and often has a broiler underneath. A range is the kitchen appliance that combines both the oven and the stove into one unit.

	Stove. Every chef's dream kitchen certainly includes a gourmet stove cooktop. Wolf commercial cooktops with 6 gas open burners are regarded as the standard for home chefs preparing high quality meals.
	Oven. The cooking can be powered by fuel (gas or propane) or by electricity. However, modern gas stoves also need electricity to power all the fancy features, such as the clock, alarm, lights, and programming.
	Range. In a gourmet kitchen, don't expect to see slide-in or freestanding ranges. Instead, double ovens, convection ovens, and custom installation ovens are the standard of luxury. Look for features such as a self-cleaning oven, an adjustable broiler, a warming drawer, and child lock-out safety feature.

	**Commercial-grade Range.** Wolf brand is respected as first class and often seen in luxury homes. With 2 ovens side by side, custom-designed cooktops feature an infrared griddle, infrared charbroiler, and/or French cooktop. Sturdy construction quality is highlighted by red signature knobs.
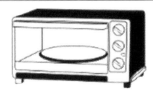	**Convection Ovens** are desirable for their quick and even cooking because it has a high-speed fan that circulates heated air as the food is being cooked. Regarded as a home cook's favorite oven, often a custom kitchen will include a convection oven for roasting.

On a stove, do the burners offer quick-boil and low-simmer settings? Does it have pilotless ignition? Do the rings lift off for authentic wok cooking? Other great features that chefs crave:

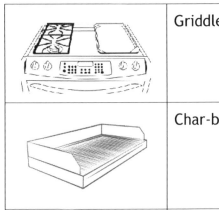	Griddle Top
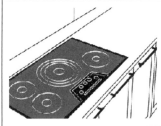	Char-broiler
	Induction electric cooktops with a smooth glass surface provide nearly instant heat for a metal pan, yet are safe to the touch for cooks. Features include multiple settings and count-down timers. Induction heating is an impressive tech advancement beyond the standard ceramic electric stovetop.

The new look includes retro appliances too! Antique ranges such Gold medal, Glenwood, and Brookline are lovingly restored to highlight their heirloom value. These one-of-a-kind vintage ranges bring unique character and charm into a kitchen, highlighting the home owner's individuality.

Clothes Washer & Clothes Dryer

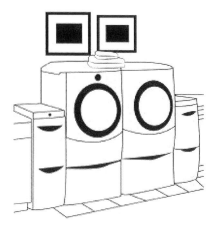

Washers

Clothes washers may be top-load, front-load, or stackable style (with the dryer). Top loading, the most common, spin the clothes in a round plastic tub. Front loading, the newer modern style, are usually more energy efficient. Stacked washer and dryer units save space, but the loads are smaller and the appliances typically cannot operate simultaneously. Features to look for include: digital display, alarm settings, quiet cycle, delayed start, and various options for steam. The washer often does not convey with the purchase of a home.

Dryers

Modern dryers are quieter, more energy efficient, and color coordinated. Features include a drying rack, timer, and various auto sensor settings. Newer front-loading models may include a pedestal to lift it higher off the ground. It helps avoid back pain from reaching over, and also may be used as a storage drawer underneath. Gas dryers are plumbed for fuel, while electric dryers need a special 220 plug. Some laundry areas are equipped for both gas and electric, so the homeowner can choose either type of dryer. The dryer often does not convey with the purchase of a home.

Other Appliances

Commercial-Grade Refrigerators - These robust appliances installed in luxury homes are wider, taller, and much heavier. The highly renowned Sub-Zero brand features water filtration, air purification, and dual-refrigeration technology behind a control console.

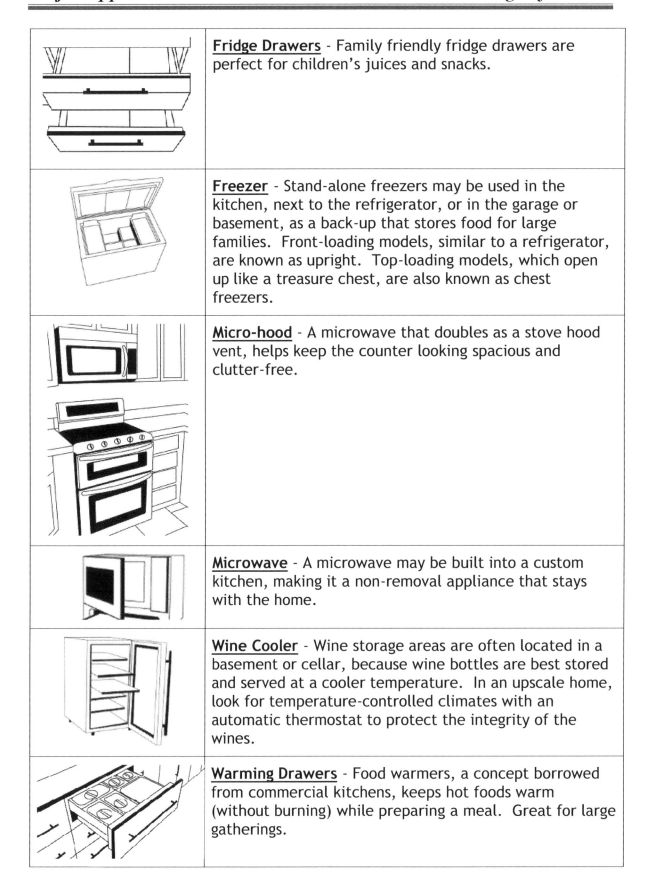

Fridge Drawers - Family friendly fridge drawers are perfect for children's juices and snacks.

Freezer - Stand-alone freezers may be used in the kitchen, next to the refrigerator, or in the garage or basement, as a back-up that stores food for large families. Front-loading models, similar to a refrigerator, are known as upright. Top-loading models, which open up like a treasure chest, are also known as chest freezers.

Micro-hood - A microwave that doubles as a stove hood vent, helps keep the counter looking spacious and clutter-free.

Microwave - A microwave may be built into a custom kitchen, making it a non-removal appliance that stays with the home.

Wine Cooler - Wine storage areas are often located in a basement or cellar, because wine bottles are best stored and served at a cooler temperature. In an upscale home, look for temperature-controlled climates with an automatic thermostat to protect the integrity of the wines.

Warming Drawers - Food warmers, a concept borrowed from commercial kitchens, keeps hot foods warm (without burning) while preparing a meal. Great for large gatherings.

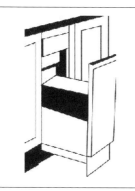	**Trash Compactor** - Trash compactors can save space by reducing the amount of trash. Some under-counter trash areas have pull-out drawers for recycled materials as well.
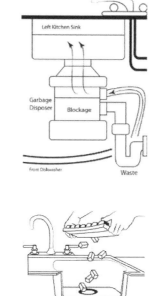	**Garbage Disposal** – shreds food so that it be easily flushed down the drain without clogging the plumbing pipes.

Conclusion

Major appliances, also known as large appliances or domestic appliances, are household machines used for cooking, food preservation, or laundry. They are not easily portable like small appliances (blenders, toasters). They are different from a plumbing fixture because they require an energy source to operate.

Eco-conscious "green" products promote energy sustainability while saving money on power bills, and Energy Star® qualified appliances can earn tax rebates. They may be considered either personal property or real property, so verify whether it will be conveying (staying with the house) when representing both sellers and buyers.

6. Fireplaces

View sample illustrations on our pinterest board:

http://www.pinterest.com/realtyproadvisr/fireplaces

What's better than a bright yellow crackling fire on a cold, rainy night? Fireplaces bring ambiance and warmth into our homes; they create a comfortable atmosphere. Wood-burning stoves are even more practical: they radiate heat, and also cook pots of food. Fireplaces are usually installed by the home builder, but can be added later. Let's learn some of the various types and their terms.

Styles

Fireplace styles include antique, colonial, contemporary, rustic, and traditional.

Antique

Vintage style fireplaces utilize original materials from period-style homes. Many historic and century-old houses boast reclaimed wood and tile, or repurposed iron and metals.

Colonial

Forged metal, strap hinged, and hand-wrought metal handles reminiscent of colonial days help define this old-fashioned style fireplace.

Contemporary

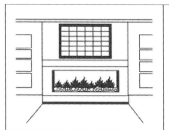

Modern homes offer the convenience of sleek-looking ash-free fireplaces. With a gas starter and ceramic logs, home owners are pleased to add an uncluttered style and warm ambiance without the maintenance.

Rustic

Bricks and hand-carved wood define this fireplace style. Other organic materials, such as rocks and mortar, add a homey country appeal.

Traditional

Traditional fireplaces are permanently installed into a wall, lined with brick interior flue. With a fire-proof hearth and wooden mantle above, it encloses a real wood fire. It may have a gas starter, or not. Surrounded by decorative wood or tile designs, the fire is constrained by glass doors and/or a wrought iron screen. Regular maintenance includes sweeping out ashes and cleaning the flue.

Stoves

A large metal box or cylinder forged from iron. With a door that opens, it stands on metal legs and has a metal flue. It can heat a whole house and cook food on its flat surface; however, the flame is not visible. Valued for its practicality, it can stand alone near a wall, in the middle of a room, or be inserted into an existing traditional fireplace. The fire is contained so there are less airborne ashes to cause allergies or lung problems. Alternative solid fuel includes coal or pellets.

Wall-Mounted

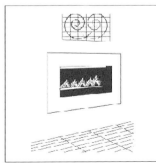

Smaller fireplace, fueled by electricity, installs in or on a wall. Fresh modern design can be easily mounted in homes with limited space because no flue is needed. It also eliminates allergies and lung problems caused by airborne ashes.

Types & Designs

Decorative Fireplace

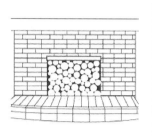

A faux fireplace that brings aesthetic value to the home but does not operate. It may be used for staging purposes, to hide a fault in a wall, or simply to add charm and character.

Double Fireplace

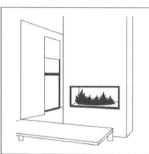

This style fireplace has openings on 2 sides, each into a different room. This luxury feature could be installed between a master bedroom and master bathroom, or between a living room and dining room.

Electric Fire

A fire that is powered with electricity rather than gas or wood-burning logs. It doesn't need a flue, so it saves space. Simulating a traditional fire, it can be installed on a wall.

Electric Heater

These fireplace look-alikes bring the ambiance and warmth yet are portable and can be place anywhere there is a power outlet. They may placed directly on the ground or in a decorative mantle-type frame. They give off heat and the temperature can be adjusted just like a regular portable heater.

Ethanol-Burning Vent-Free

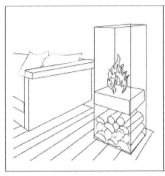

A natural biofuel, denatured ethanol does not require a metal pipe connected to utilities. Allergy and asthma sufferers enjoy the lack of ashes and airborne particles that come from burning wood. Because it doesn't have a vent, the heat stays and warms the room. A wonderful solution for condos, they can be installed on ledges, built into walls, or be free-standing. Check out GREEN solutions from EcoSmart.

Masonry Heater / Radiant Fireplace

As a primary heat source for rural homes, masonry heaters are built in a home's central location and fired up only once per day. The system captures the heat and disburses it in the house throughout the day. May be connected to an HVAC radiant system, such as floors and hot water tank. These enormous styles may feature hand-crafted stonework and carved sitting benches. This "heart of the home" is often a design element in the center of the home. Some masonry fireplaces even include pizza-baking ovens.

Open Fire

An open fire that is NOT enclosed in a fireplace. It may burn wood coal, or solid fuels such as gas or ethanol. Instead of a traditional-looking chimney, it has a canopy hood that draws smoke up and out of the house. This ultra-modern design may be seen in upscale and luxury homes.

Oversized Fireplace

An extended opening allows this extra-large fireplace to burn an open fire, often with sitting benches for family to gather around. It takes up an entire wall of the room.

Smokeless Fireplace

Fireplaces that use electricity or burn environmentally friendly gel fuel. Because they don't produce smoke or ashes, they are considered safer for those with allergies or asthma.

Stoves

Iron stoves are more efficient when burning using combustion because they rely on outdoor air intake. They are often a good option for those looking to convert to a GREEN energy efficient house without indoor air pollution.

Insert Fireplace

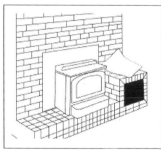

An enclosed metal firebox that sits inside of a traditional fireplace opening. Usually these are inserted afterwards as an adaptation to the existing fireplace. They can burn wood logs, pellets, or coal. Doors may be clear glass or solid metal.

Multi-Fuel Stove

Can burn wood, coal, pellets, and/or smokeless fuel. A solid fuel stove burns wood, coal, or pellets. This stove can be installed inside of a traditional fireplace opening and often connects to the existing flue and chimney.

Pot-Belly Stove

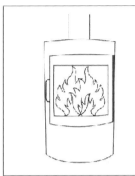	A wood-burning stove is that round shaped and can be installed in the corner of a room.

Wood Burning Stove

	A metal stove that burns wooden logs. May also burn other solid fuels such as coal or pellets.

Materials

Add texture and character to a fireplace by combining the following materials:

- Brick
- Cultured stone – cast concrete that resembles natural stone
- Faux stone / rock
- Forged Metal
- Glass tile
- Marble
- Rock
- Stone
- Stacked Stone
- Stone Veneer (artificial stone look)
- Tile – especially natural travertine
- Wrought iron

Parts & Features

This section covers the many fireplace parts.

Ashpan

A flat, metal pan inserted under the fire which collects the burned ashes. It can be pulled out for ease of emptying the ashes and cleaning the fireplace.

Chimney

The tall brick tunnel above the fireplace that is built around the flue pipe. Usually built into an exterior wall, the brick is often visible from the exterior. Chimneys may service multiple fireplaces; for example, 2nd floor fireplace may be located directly above the 1st floor fireplace and utilize the same flue. The chimney may be decorative as well as functional.

Chimney Stack

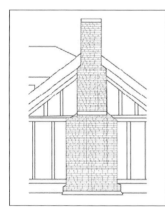

The portion of the brick chimney that rises above the roofline.

Cleanout

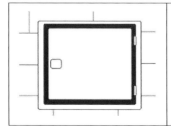

The fireplace cleanout is a small heavy metal door in the back of the chimney. It opens for rapid removal of the ashes, often more efficient than removing ashes from the front and carrying them through the house.

Collar

On a wood-burning stove, the flue spigot at the stove top in which the vitreous pipe is inserted.

Doors - Glass

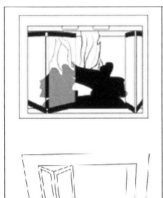

Just like screens, they protect the home from fire damage caused by flying sparks and ashes. They also help to regulate the heat coming from the fire. For families with children, glass doors are a safety feature, preventing youngsters from touching the fire. Glass doors may swing open or push back accordion-style.

Fireback

A large cast iron, concrete, metal, or brick plate in the back of the fireplace. Its purpose is to redirect heat from the fireplace and radiate the heat into the room. Firebacks may add a decorative element.

Firebox

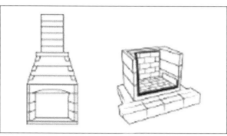

The area inside of the fireplace which contains the fire. It is constructed of fire-proof brick or other similar materials.

Flue

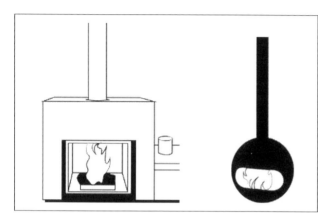

A long, tall metal pipe above the fire that allows smoke and gases from a fireplace to ventilate to the outside. The flue is usually contained inside of a brick chimney. It may have a liner (a stainless steel flexible tube).

Chimney Sweep

The flue needs to be cleaned periodically to remove the build-up of creosote, which can become flammable, and to clear the debris so the flue can operate effectively. A chimney sweep with a special broom can clean the flue.

Cowl

A metal cover installed on top of a chimney flue that allows smoke to escape but prevents birds and rain from entering the flue. Look for the anti-downdraft version.

Gas Starter

Metal pipe carries gas fuel into the fireplace. A starter on the side of the fireplace turns the gas on or off. Its main purpose is to start or burn a wood fire. It can also be used as a stand-alone fire for ambiance (not for heat, as a gas fire does not get as hot as a wood-burning fire).

Grate

A heavy iron metal stand made of iron fingers. It elevates the wood logs above the floor of the fireplace to stimulate airflow.

Hearth

The space in front of a fireplace, installed with fire-resistance materials such as brick, tile, or stone. It may be placed directly on the floor, or it may be a ledge that people can sit upon. Often the fireplace utensils (broom, tray, poker) and the wood may sit on the hearth.

Mantle

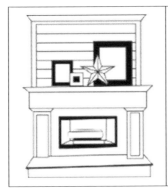

A large, wooden decorative shelf above the fireplace. Styles range from basic rustic wood to elaborate carved framework. May also be constructed of stone, tile, or brick.

Register Plate

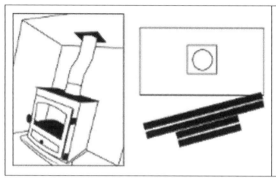

A stainless steel or galvanized metal plate fitted inside the flue. Its purpose is to seal the chimney in cases when the flue does not have a liner. Not to be confused with a closure plate or cover plate.

Screens (Wrought Iron)

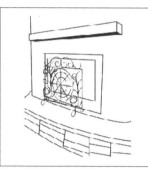

Metal screens contain the ashes and prevent sparks from flying into the room. They also help the fireplace to emit steady heat rather than spurts of heat from wood burning. Wrought iron designs accent gorgeous styles. They are used for durability and also aesthetic charm. Metal screens may be pull-type permanently installed curtains, or portable frames.

Throat

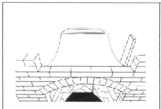

The "neck" where the fireplace narrows to meet the flue.

Tool Set

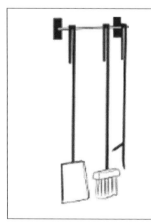

A fireplace tool set typically includes a small shovel to remove ashes, a poker to manipulate hot logs in the fireplace, and a broom to clean the hearth.

Conclusion

With so many convenient options, every homeowner can enjoy the mood of a glowing fireplace on a cold wintry night. Remember when your buyers are purchasing a home with a fireplace, they may opt to have a fireplace inspection. And when sellers are selling a house, they should have the fireplace cleaned and serviced, and provide a copy of the receipt to the buyers. Unless, of course, it's a faux fireplace!

7. Lighting

View sample illustrations on our pinterest board:

http://www.pinterest.com/realtyproadvisr/lighting

"Let there be light" and, almost as importantly, let there be attractive light fixtures! They set the tone, define the style, and magnify the home's ambiance. Today's article about lighting defines fixtures you can highlight when advertising your new listing. And as a buyer's agent, help your clients identify the light fixtures when viewing homes.

Ceiling Lights

Lights above us embellish the entry way, living room, and bedrooms. From chandeliers to pendants, they bring beauty into the home. And what about those lights doing double duty as a fan or skylight.

Chandelier

	A chandelier is an elegant hanging light fixture with multiple lamps and diverse designs. Constructed of metal, they often feature crystal hanging from the lamps. Chandeliers are most often seen in dining rooms.

Crystal Chandelier

	A crystal chandelier is comprised of glamorous sparkling crystal "teardrops" and other exotic shapes hanging from the chandelier. It drips luxury.

Mini-Chandeliers

 Mini-chandeliers are vogue for a modern, chic style. With a concept similar to chandeliers but on a smaller scale, they create a luxury effect in bathrooms and bedrooms.

Entryway / Foyer

 A foyer or entryway light is the first thing you see when opening the front doors. Hanging from the ceiling, it brings ambiance and a welcoming spirit to a home, and sets the style tone.

Pendant Lights

 A pendant light is a single lamp in a decorative setting that hangs from the ceiling. It's often a glass and metal fixture, but can be plastic or other materials. Style statements can be traditional, modern, rustic, or artistic.

Close to Ceiling

 The standard light fixture that is mounted directly on the ceiling is called "close to ceiling". They can be half-spheres, squares, or other shapes. Also known as "flush mount" style.

Track Lighting

 Popular in the 80's, track lighting is a metal strip mounted across the ceiling. Several slideable lamps are installed on a track. The lamps can be moved back and forth along the track.

Swag Lamp

 A swag light hangs from the ceiling by a metal chain intertwined with the electrical cord. The long chain/cord anchored to a 2nd spot on the ceiling, near the wall, and then drapes down to the light plug at the bottom of the wall. These lights were popular in 60's and 70's bedrooms, where the light switches were connected to the electric plugs rather than overhead lights. AKA plug-in swag light.

Plug-In Swag

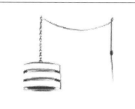 Designed for rooms with no overhead electrical connection, these swag light fixtures hang from the ceiling with hooks. The chain with the electric cord is plugged into a wall outlet. Popular style amongst 60's & 70's homes because of the lack of ceiling lights.

Fan Lights

 Fan lights perform double duty as both light sources and airflow circulation. Fans have 3 or 4 paddles that swirl and operate independently of the lamp. Modern fan lights have a remote control switch rather than a metal chain on the fan. Some models spin in one direction for cool air, but generate heat when operated in the opposite direction. They can be installed as either hugger flush mount or drop-down. Energy efficient models are also available.

Skylight / Light Combo

 Ceiling-to-roof fixtures that bring natural sunshine during daylight hours can also have a light fixture inside. During nighttime hours, the light is switched on. Can be a dome skylight or a solar tube.

Kitchen Lighting

Ambient lighting in the kitchen draws in family and guests when the chef is cooking. It also illuminates those colorful dishes of food being prepared.

Kitchen Island Lights

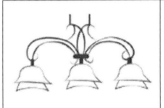

A kitchen island light is a hanging fixture specially designed to illuminate a rectangular island table. Boasting multiple small lamps, it brings a decorative quality to the kitchen and dining room design.

Fluorescent Tube Lights

Long fluorescent tubes are enclosed in a stand-alone plain rectangular fixture or a wooden rectangular box. This lighting was popular in kitchens and bathrooms built in the 80's & 90's.

Recessed Fluorescent Lights (in Drop-Down Ceiling)

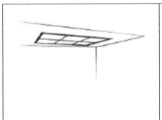

Long fluorescent tube lights are mounted within a box flush mounted in a drop-down ceiling. They are often in a series of 2 – 4 light boxes. Vinyl panels covered can be replaced with patterned panels, such as blue sky with clouds mural or the "look" of ornamental scrolled iron, or stained glass.

Decorative Rod Fixture

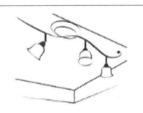

A long, curvy decorative rod is adorned with several lamps. The lamps are permanently affixed to the rod, not slideable track lighting. However, the lamps can be pointed in various positions.

Mini-Pendant Lights

A small single lamp hanging from the ceiling in a simple decorative shell. Often shaped as a cone, tear drop, or cylinder, they are usually set in a row of 3 to echo a theme. Popular above a breakfast bar or kitchen peninsula.

Recessed Round Lights

 Also known as "pot lights" or "can lights", these special-type bulbs are inside of a metal sleeve and inserted into the ceiling. They are mounted flush with the ceiling to provide spot lights in a certain area. Usually installed in a pattern of multiple lights and most often seen in kitchens.

Under Cabinet Lights

 Designed for kitchens, these small, multiple lights are mounted underneath kitchen cabinets. They shine light on work areas for cooks in the kitchen. They can be electric powered, battery operated, or LED bulbs.

LED Portable Lights

 LED individual disc lights save energy. They can be mounted under cabinets, in closets, or used as night lights.

Wall Lights

Permanently installed lights mounted on the walls can bring warmth and style to a home's décor.

Wall Lamps

 Wall lamps are mounted directly on the wall. A variety of styles and shapes help beautify the home and lend a mellow ambiance.

Sconces

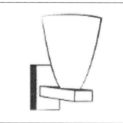 Sconces are small, single lamps in a decorative shell attached directly to the wall. They are usually in pairs and often seen in an entry way, hallway, or each side of a bed. Sconces are crafted from chrome, bronze, or brushed steel. They can be LED-lit to save energy.

Swing Arm Wall Lamps

 Popular in earlier generations, a swing arm wall lamp is mounted directly on the wall. With an accordion-type arm, it can be pulled out for versatility, or pushed back against the wall when not in use.

Picture Lights

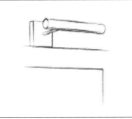 A picture light is a long, single lamp in a decorative metal finish installed above a mounted frame. It highlights photos or art collections.

Bathroom Lights

Light up the smallest room in the house with specialty lights designed just for the bathroom.

Bathroom Vanity Lights

 Single-lamp wall sconces installed in pairs above bathroom vanities or beside mirrors. Can also be a 2-lamp vanity light.

Vanity Strip Lighting

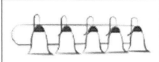 Bathroom mirror strip lights are installed against the wall, directly above the mirror. Usually an oak or metal plate with multiple lamps (typically 3, 4, or 5). Feature round bulbs or glass shades that open either upwards or downwards. Various styles reflect the era of the home.

Bathroom Fan / Light Combo

A ceiling mounted light that doubles as a fan. Primarily used for ventilation in bathrooms, the fixture has a grille to allow air flow and a blower assembly hidden in the ceiling.

Heat Lamp

A heat lamp is a large high-wattage ceiling lamp used primarily in bathrooms to keep it dry, which deters mold and mildew. Popular in the 60's and 70's, modern versions include a combination fixture — heat lamps with a fan and a regular light.

Exterior Lighting

On the porch and patio, homeowners can enjoy soft exterior lighting around their home, especially here with San Diego's mild climate all year long. Bright security lights also protect residents.

Porch Lights

These lanterns are permanently affixed to the exterior wall of the home, right next to the front door. A porch light adorns the home with welcoming light in the evenings and creates dynamic curb appeal. Can be LED energy efficient lighting and may also have a motion sensor or a trigger.

Ceiling Lights

Outdoor ceiling lights are specially designed to withstand moisture. They are mounted directed onto the ceiling of a porch or patio.

Outdoor Fan Light

 These functional fan lights are designed to be installed in semi-outdoor rooms, such as patios and porches. They effectively help prevent mildew and mold through the air circulation which dries out damp rooms.

Post Lights

 Post lights sit atop fence posts around the exterior of the yard. They brighten walk ways, driveways, and gardens.

Motion/Security Lights

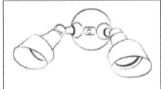 Security lights are extremely high wattage bright lights installed in key locations on the home's exterior. They turn on when motion is detected, making them ideal for safety because they deter intruders. AKA Flood Lights.

Hanging Lights

 These lanterns hang outside on the porch or entryway. Can also be used for indoor/outdoor living space, such as a lanai.

Rope Lighting

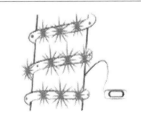 Rope lighting is a long narrow clear tube with tiny lamps inside the sleeve. The rope is flexible for installation along a variety of surfaces. It works well underneath cabinets, above baseboard, on stair steps, and along tray ceiling molding. With low-energy LED lights, they light up a dark space in a novel way and can be used outdoors.

String Lights

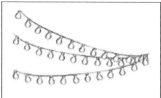

String lights are multiple mini-lamps, each encased in a decorative shell, connected to each other via a long cord. The light fixture is installed along the side of a building, underneath a patio or arbor, or simply strung across the yard.

Shop Lights

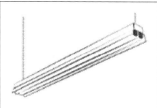

Designed for workshops, these long, rectangular lights hang from the ceiling by 2 chains and contain fluorescent lamps. Designed to withstand damp locations, these industrial style lights are usually found hanging over a workbench in a garage or shop.

Landscape Lighting

Homeowners who invest their effort into beautiful trees, flowers, and hardscaping should show off their elegant designs with landscape lights.

Spotlights

These small low-voltage lights have a post inserted in the ground and they often bend to various angles. They highlight elegant landscaping and brighten garden areas.

Dark Sky

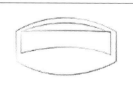

A dark sky light is a cool techy design that illuminates the ground on either side; the lights are mounted on the ground to light a walkway. Light projects out the sides rather than the top. Available in many styles, these Dark Sky compliant designs light the ground, not the sky.

Path Lights

Path lights are lamps on stakes inserted into the ground next to walkways. They guide the outdoor paths in the evenings. They can be solar powered, battery powered, or wired with electric cords buried under the soil. May be on a programmed timer or an automatic switch.

Well Lights

Round plastic cylinders inserted in the ground with a low-voltage lamp shining straight up. Lights up trees and other landscaping. Some lights rotate and come in optional bright colors to produce interesting effects.

Light Bricks

These brick-shaped glass tiles include a lighting assembly that gets recessed into a walkway, a brick wall, or a deck. These extremely effective floor-mounted lights withstand the weight of people walking on them. Also called "light steps" or "light tiles", they are often solar powered so they don't need electricity.

Stair Lights / Deck Lights

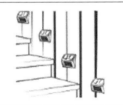

Stair lights are small lamps that light each step of an outdoor staircase. Functional walkway lights help people find their way home — even in the dark. They are usually solar powered so they don't need electric cords.

Solar Powered

Solar powered lights save energy because they gather their energy from the sun during the day. They are used atop fence posts, in-ground to light walkways, and planted amongst landscaping. Most any type of outdoor light can be solar powered.

Lamp Shade Styles

Some interesting lamp shades are listed below. Hundreds of varieties can be created from lighting hardware and accessories, including one-of-a-kind custom designs.

Drum

	A drum lampshade is a short cylinder-shaped design. Cloth or heat-resistant vinyl can be used as the shade. Drum lampshades can be used for hanging lights, as well as portable lamps, for a crisp contemporary style.

Glass

	A glass pendant lamp is a semi-sphere shaped upside-down bowl that hangs from the ceiling.

Giclee

	Giclee is a modern look that sports a hand-painted or artistic material lamp shade. They can be custom made. Each style is unique and individual to suit the home's décor.

Industrial

	Industrial styled lights are crafted from shiny silver and fashioned with construction-quality touches. They can be used in the kitchen, den, office, or any room with a silver metal look.

Conclusion

Light draws people in. It signals comfort and security, such as the Thomas Kinkade paintings. When listing a house for sale, be sure there are plenty of lights and that the bulbs are working. If not, replace the bulbs before your first open house so your listing attracts buyers and sells quickly. And, when showing homes to buyers, be sure to point out the wonderful light fixtures that brighten their new home sweet home.

8. Windows

View sample illustrations on our pinterest board:

http://www.pinterest.com/realtyproadvisr/windows

The view, the vista, the vision... a beautiful house includes a stunning view. "Our listing has a view of the valley and hills!" View of the vineyard. Breathtaking view of the ocean and seascape. So let's shine up those windows while we learn the window lingo. When our clients ask us, "Which window frames that fabulous view?" we can answer with confidence and certainty.

We'll show you various types of windows and their related accessories. What window affords a panoramic view of the scenery? Wonder which types of windows are which? Below are some phrases you may see at a caravan or hear at an open house. Become familiar with these buzz words and position yourself as the industry expert!

Window Types

Listed below are common windows that we observe while working out in the field. It seems there's no single "standard window". Who knew there were so many types of windows?

Awning Window

	A horizontally-shaped casement window that is hinged on top. The panel (sash) swings outward. When opened, the shape resembles an awning, hence its name. Traditional awning windows are often found on older buildings and can lend charm and character.

Bay Window

	A series of 3 or more window panels that project out of the main floor space into a separate "bay". They are installed at angles and form a polygon shape protruding from the wall area. "Oriel" is a type of bay window found in Tudor-style homes, but instead of extending to the ground, the windows are supported by corbels or brackets.

Bow Window

A bay window with a twist: instead of the windows set at angles, they are curved. Typically consists of a series of 4 or more windows arranged in an arch pattern. More expensive architecture than bay windows, often hand-crafted by local artisans.

Casement Window

The panel (sash) opens by turning a crank on the hinged side, and the sash swings either in or out. Although a casement window may be top-hung or bottom-hung, it is most often installed as side-hung.

Clerestory Window

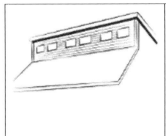
Roof-level windows that allow light into the room. These windows, placed above eye level, provide privacy and daylight while reducing the need for electric powered lights. Although a recent trend towards green energy has fueled the demand for passive solar light, clerestory windows originated from traditional European churches. Also known as clearstorey, clearstory, or overstorey windows.

Dormer Window

Set into the sides of a roof, a dormer window provides light and sometimes ventilation for attics and top floors in a multi-level home. They also provide additional headroom and a more open floor plan for upper stories.

Double-Hung Window

 A window with 2 sashes placed vertically, and each sash is able to be opened. The most typical style is a glider window; both upper and lower panes slide up and down. An alternate style is when sashes are hinged on the bottom and open outward on the top of each sash.

Traditional homes built before 1960 will often feature double-hung windows. Compare to Single-Hung Windows.

Fanlight Window

 A half-circle window shaped like a fan with "spokes" radiating from the center. Fanlight windows do not open, because they are used as decorative windows over doors or other windows.

French Window

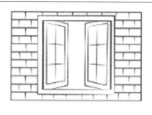 A pair of 2 panels (sashes) hinged on the right and left sides of the window, and both panels open to the middle. This creates a "French door" effect. The window is latched in the middle. May have a lattice pattern. Sometimes a French door that overlooks a patio or terrace is referred to as a French window.

Glider / Sliding Window

 Window with a gliding sash (window panel) that slides back and forth to open and close. May slide horizontally or vertically, although horizontal sliding is more typical. Gliders are the most common types of modern windows in new construction.

Louvre Window

A window comprised of parallel glass or acrylic horizontal slats which may open and close. They are angled with a downward slope to deflect rain and wind, but allow indirect sunlight. Also known as a jalousie window, louvre windows are often found in tropical homes.

Picture Window

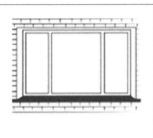

An extra-large window that provides a broad outside view and lets in a lot of light. Picture windows are usually non-opening (inoperable) windows. Often single paned and typically do not contain any glazing bars which may mar the fabulous view. They are called "picture" windows because the large window is intended to provide a wide view of the outdoors, similar to a picture frame.

Single-Hung Window

A window with 2 panels (sashes), arranged vertically to each other, wherein the top panel is fixed and the bottom panel opens. It may open by sliding up, or at the top (if it is hinged on the bottom). Single-hung windows were the original style of windows installed in the early 1900's before double-hung windows were devised. Compare to Double-Hung Window.

Stained Glass Window / Leaded

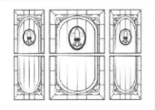

Small pieces of leaded glass separated by lead glazing bars. Frequently seen in Victorian era homes, stained glass pieces are arranged in a pattern or architectural style. Stained glass windows are hand-crafted and difficult to replace. They are valued for their character and artistry.

Transom Window

A window installed above other windows, or above a door opening. It may be either an external or an internal window. The main purpose of a transom window is to bring light into a room, so it is usually a fixed window which is not operable. However, some transom windows open on hinges to allow ventilation between rooms. A transom window may be a decorative style technique.

Construction & Accessories

Windows need hardware to operate, and charming accessories add character to the home. As you're inspecting the home and explaining it to your clients, you may also need to know some of the basic construction components of the windows. Don't worry, we've got you covered!

Bars

Metals bars installed across a window for safety and security. Often arranged together as a decorative wrought iron pattern. Prospective buyers viewing homes with bars across the windows, may perceive the home as being located in an unsafe neighborhood with high crime.

Blinds Built in

A luxurious type of window that contains horizontal mini-blinds encased between the 2 dual panes of a window. Blinds are opened and closed via a slide knob on the side of the window. These types of windows are popular because the blinds are never damaged, they stay in perfect condition without bending, rusting, or collecting dust. These windows are preferred by folks who strive for a dust-free home without allergens.

Dual Pane

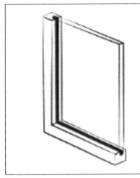

Two glass panes of glass separated by air or invisible gas material. The purpose of dual pane windows is to insulate the building by not allowing heat or cold to escape through the windows. The insulating gas frequent used between the 2 panes is "argon". (Note: compare to single pane window)

Fixed (non-operable)

Windows that are not able to be opened for ventilation are called "fixed". The purpose of a non-operational window is to allow sunlight into a room, or to give a view of the outside.

Flashing

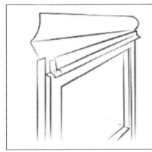

A piece of metal or other material, installed on top of the window and around the edges. Its purpose is to prevent water damage from the window by forming a barrier shield around the window. Windows without flashing can suffer from dry rot, termite infestation, and damage to the walls.

Frame

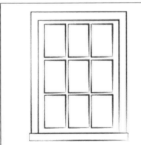

The wood or metal exterior of a window pane which holds the entire panel in place.

Grilles

 Grilles are bars of wood or vinyl that separate the window into smaller squares, or that give the appearance of several smaller windows. GBG = "grilles between the glass".

Hardware

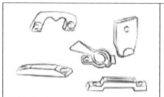 Hardware includes metal and other window accessory parts, such as hinges, pulleys, pivots, locks, fasteners, lifts, and pivots.

Header

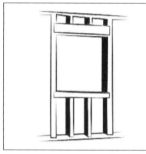 The wood support beam above a window. The header beam is larger than most of the other beams. Its purpose is to provide the building with strong support around window openings. If the header is cut, it may compromise the integrity of the building.

Jamb

 Sides and top of a window framing that support the opening structurally. May be part of the interior window trim.

Lintel

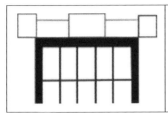

A horizontal stone or beam across the top of a window, designed as an architectural ornament. It may also function as a load bearing beam.

Low E Glass

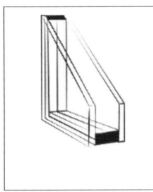

For "Greenies" seeking an energy-efficient home, the Low E Glass features low emissivity, which reduces infra-red rays and reduces ultra-violet light. They help to protect carpet and furniture from fading. These windows are often used for large south-facing window which receive a lot of direct sunlight. Another similar type of glass is Passive Solar (Low-E 180). These windows are premium products which are slightly more expensive than regular windows.

Sash

A window panel that is able to be opened, typically a sliding glass panel. Can be framed with wood, vinyl, metal, or fiberglass.

Screen

A fine metal mesh panel, inserted behind a window, which allows ventilation through open windows but keeps the insects from entering.

Shutters

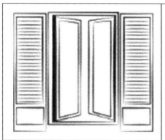 Window shutters are wood louvers, either decorative that frame a window, or functional that close to block light from a room. Some shutters are doubled on each side, and swing to close with hinges in between each pair.

Sill

 A wooden, stone, or manufactured material that goes across the bottom of the window opening and forms the window base. The sill can be inside, outside, or both. The slat should slope away from the window to keep water and moisture from damaging the window.

Storm Windows

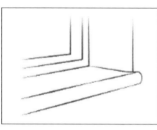 A window specially designed to protect the occupants against tornados, hurricanes, and other severe, stormy weather. Often seen in southeast homes and in Atlantic tropical locations.

Tempered Glass

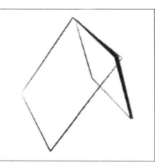 Manufactured so that if it breaks, there are no jagged edges. It's safer and in case of emergency, people will not be hurt easily. Most building safety codes require low windows to have tempered glass.

Trim

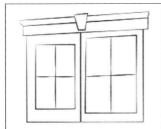 Decorative material around a window which is also practical for insulation around the window, both exterior and interior. Trim can be made with wood, vinyl, or factory-created materials. Adding architectural quality trim is a simple way to update the décor and curb appeal of a home.

Vinyl Windows

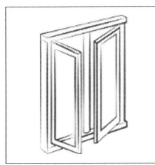 Windows that are encased in vinyl (often white) rather than traditional metal or wood. Vinyl is used more frequently because it is affordable, durable, and does not deteriorate as quickly. Most newer vinyl windows are dual-paned glass with high energy efficiency ratings.

Conclusion

Who knew there were so many window types? Now that you know the difference between Bay Windows and Bow Windows, low E glass and tempered glass, you can impress your clients!

So shine those windows squeaky clean and let that fabulous view be the star of the show. Remember: the better the view, the higher the value!

9. Doors

View sample illustrations on our pinterest board:

http://www.pinterest.com/realtyproadvisr/doors-interior-exterior

When your seller's house has beautiful master-crafted hardwood doors, brag about it in your listing! Unique doors demonstrate a touch of originality and will attract discriminating buyers with impeccable taste. Or, if the doors are functional and economical, that's okay too. As long as you know which is which.

When taking a listing, how do you describe exquisite and unusual custom doors? When viewing a listing with your buyers, can you determine whether the doors are robust and high quality?

EXTERIOR DOORS

What's better than a door that declares "Welcome to our home!" A door is the access way into a home. But doors do more than provide access. Doors announce a grand entrance; they insulate our houses; they provide safety and security by shutting out the world; and they can add exquisite beauty.

An exterior door secures the inside of a house and protects its residents from weather and intruders. Exterior doors include front entry doors, protective doors, patio doors, and back doors.

Entry Doors

Front doors lend character to a home's architectural style. They can offer stunning curb appeal that improves the property value. Our front door, adorned with a door knocker and a mat, welcomes guests to our home.

Standard Door

	Larger and heavier than an interior door, a standard front door size is the rectangular 36 inches wide by 80 inches tall. It's usually constructed of solid wood and may feature "lights" (glass window pane inserts), a brass door knocker, or a peephole. Homes built before 1960 often have a mail slot in the door. Heavy-duty metal doors are a good alternative to solid wood construction.
	"Single Door" means there is 1 door, and "Double Doors" means 2 doors side by side that swing open in the middle. Quality doors feature raised panels and glass lights arranged in a pattern.

Tops

	Door tops can be curved or arched for ambiance, or may boast an elegant gothic top. Above the door of luxury homes, look for a transom (non-opening) window, a fanlight, or gorgeous decorative wood panels.

Sidelights

 Sidelights are the tall, narrow glass panels on each side of the door that add aesthetic value and highlight a beautiful entry way. Doors may feature just 1 sidelight, or a set of 2 (on either side of the door). Sidelights often reflect the patterns on the door.

Oversized Door

 An oversized door is taller, and often wider, than a standard door. Intricate carvings, a wrought iron grill, and wood straps can make a front door the focus of a home's architecture style. For example, a Mission style home may be enhanced with a beautiful solid oak door of 8 feet or taller.

Wicket Door

 A wicket door is an oversized door with a standard-sized entrance door inside of it. The purpose is to grant access to the building easily without opening the entire oversized door.

Cultural & Custom Styles

 A luxury home will feature imported hand-crafted solid wood, custom-made doors, and may borrow its architectural style from a far-flung culture. Look for interesting designs that grace a building by drawing on cultural inspirations.

Refer to the following list for various cultural and ethnic door styles.

Some of the cultural door styles include colorful designs such as:

- Arabic
- Arts & Crafts
- Italian Renaissance
- Japanese

- Barcelona
- Barn Door
- Celtic
- Egyptian
- Gothic
- Irish

- Ledge & Brace
- Medieval
- Mediterranean
- Shaker
- Spanish Colonial
- Tuscan

Protective Doors

Protective doors are installed in front of entry doors and offer another layer of protection and security, or simply keep flies and mosquitos away.

Screen door

	A screen door has a fine metal or fiberglass mesh that allows air circulation and light, but keeps insects and pests from entering. Screen doors can be hinged on the side, or they can slide back (such as patio doors). Retractable screen doors, which "disappear" out of sight, operate with spring-loaded rollers and a magnetic clip closing.

Metal Security Door

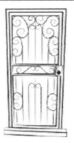	Security doors are a first line of defense to shield residents. When buyers see a home with traditional steel metal bars on the doors and windows, they may question the safety of the neighborhood. So, newer door designs complement the home's style, rather than detract from it, with gorgeous wrought iron charm.

Storm Door

Popular in areas with hostile weather, storm doors are made from metal and tempered glass. Some also include a sliding glass window with a screen for ventilation. Besides guarding against rain and snow, they help increase energy efficiency.

Patio Doors

Patios perfect for entertaining are often framed by glass French doors, sliding / gliding doors, or folding doors.

French Doors

A set of 2 doors, opening on the inside and hinged on the outside of each door. Glass panel inserts provide natural light and open into a back yard, patio, or garden. Fancy doors may flaunt an arched top, leaded glass inserts, or carved wood patterns. French doors add a romantic touch when opening onto a balcony (think: Romeo & Juliet).

Glass Doors

A standard glass door is simply a standard size back door in a wooden frame with a large glass panel insert. Newer versions are insulated, dual paned glass and may include blinds in the middle of the glass.

Gliding / Sliding Door

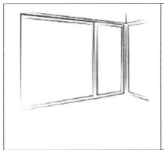	Sliding doors, also known as gliding doors, lead from a bedroom, dining room, or family room out to the patio in the back yard. This is a set of 2 wide doors, usually glass door panels framed in aluminum, wood, or vinyl. The standard height is 80" to 82" and common widths are 6 feet (72") or 8 feet (96"). A sliding door set includes a sliding screen door.

Folding Door

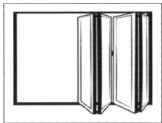	A 2- or 3-door system that folds up accordion-style. Often the door sections are wood-framed glass panels. Contemporary designs can be beautifully finished to highlight the architectural style of the house.

Sliding Folding

	These amazing doors allow full indoor/outdoor living by blurring the line between them. 2 or more door sections (on each side) fold up accordion-style and disappear into the side of the house. This stunning design is popular in luxury homes.

Back Doors

Standard exterior doors accessed from the back (or side) of a house are known as "back doors". Just like front entry doors, back doors are usually 36" wide x 80" tall and made of metal or solid wood.

Window-in-Door

Many back doors have sliding windows in the top half of the door. This allows parents to watch their children playing in the back yard. Look for easy-care inset blinds sandwiched in between the 2 glass sides.

Pet Door

A pet door is simply a regular door with a small rubber flap inset near the bottom of the door. Popular for residents with cats or dogs, these "doggie doors" can also be a glass panel that's aligned with a sliding glass door. Popular tech doors include a pet collar that restricts access, and a door that slides up to open.

Cellar Door

Set of heavy steel (or wooden) doors that face the ground. The doors lead downstairs to a weather-proof underground cellar to keep residents safe from extreme weather. Popular in the South and Mid-West due to hurricanes and tornados (think of Dorothy from the Wizard of Oz). AKA "Bulkhead"

INTERIOR DOORS

Inside a home, doors separate rooms and grant privacy. Doors reduce noise and hide unsightly messes. Doors are sometimes used to "make a point" by slamming them!

The standard height of an interior door is generally the same as an exterior door: 80" or 81". However, the standard width of an interior door is 28" or 30" which is narrower than an exterior door. Sub-standard dimensions for a manufactured home on an older house may be merely 24" wide.

Homes that were built earlier than 1950 may have odd sized doors. Before uniform building codes were implemented, doors were individually made, especially in the older Victorian homes.

Door Quality

The quality of an interior door is judged by several factors:

- Is it solid or hollow-core? Solid wood construction is heavier and more expensive; an indication of higher quality. Hollow core is made from high-density fiberboard and is less sturdy. For example, when you see a fist hole punched in a door, you know that was a hollow core door.

- Is it flush (flat) or does it have panels? Are the panels raised, flat, or inset? Paneled doors, such as the common 2-panel and 6-panel designs, demonstrate a higher caliber of quality than a flat door. Not only are paneled doors more attractive, but they are also more durable.

- Interior door hardware includes metal hinges on the side, a metal door knob (may or may not lock), and a door stop to prevent the knob from making a hole in the wall when it swings completely open. Hardware may be plain (silver) or fancy, such as oil-rubbed bronze, which magnifies the quality of a door.

- Custom doors use exotic hardwoods, such as Brazilian Mahogany, with hand-carved trim. An arched top is another sign of luxury.

Pre-hung doors include a jamb around the sides and top, and most doors are framed out by a header board at the top.

Interior Room Doors

Let's take a look at the various types of interior room doors.

Saloon Doors (AKA Café Doors)

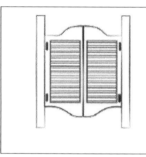 | A set of two doors, each hinged on opposite sides of the doorway. They use bi-directional hinges to swing both ways and they meet in the middle with no knob or locking mechanism. Saloon Doors often have a country western style and may echo doors found in a bar. Short doors that cover the middle length of the door are called **Batwing Doors**.

Pocket Door

 | A Pocket Door opens by sliding into a recess in the wall, rather than swinging into a room from side hinges. These types of doors are used when space is at a premium and privacy is not paramount, such as the door between the master bedroom and the master bathroom.

Dutch Door

 | A type of door that has 2 halves (top and bottom), which open independently of the other. They are hinged on the side to swing open in the same direction. Often, the top of the door is opened to allow light, air, and noise; while the bottom remains closed to keep children inside (or pets outside). Sometimes the bottom half of the door has a shelf on top of it. Traditionally, it was handy for cooling pies fresh baked from the oven.

Gliding Door

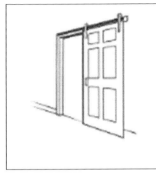

Have you seen the rustic "barn door" gliding doors made from salvaged wood? A gliding interior door uses hooks to hang from a horizontal rod above the door way, and slides across the rod to open. The door may be frosted glass or wood panels, and doesn't lock or have a doorknob. Its purpose is typically for room separation and aesthetics, so it doesn't provide much privacy; for example, a room divider.

Closet Doors

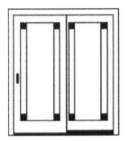

Below are 2 types of closet doors most frequently seen in houses.

Sliding Closet Doors

These are the most common type of closet doors. They are flush or raised-panel doors with rollers installed at the top. The rollers guide the doors open along a horizontal track above, with guides at the bottom of the doors. They may have mirrored panels to give the illusion of a larger room. Closet doors are often installed in pairs that slide in front of each other.

Bi-fold Door

A door with 2 or more long, vertical sections hinged to each other. It opens by folding up accordion-style against the sides of the closet. A pair of bi-fold doors are can also hide a laundry area. Usually constructed of wood louvers for ventilation, they don't lock or provide much privacy.

Innovative Doors

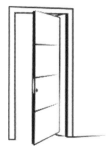

Doors can be an artist's canvas for creativity. Innovative doors include the evolution door, vento door, and door of secrets as shown below. To get a closer look at these unique doors, refer to our pinterest site shown at the beginning of this chapter.

Evolution Door

	Space-age "Evolution" door looks like it's straight from the Jetsons cartoon. Similar to an origami design, 4 triangular panels split, flip across, and re-assemble themselves. This new-age door is artistic and fascinating to watch. Also known as a "Flip Panel Door".

Vento Door

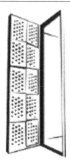	This door is fabricated from 10 blocks with holes to allow for air ventilation; hence the name "vento". The pragmatic design combines the convenience of storage as each "block" doubles as a magazine rack! With magazines in each slot, the door is private; without magazines, it's translucent. Constructed from Baltic birch plywood or eco-friendly recycled plastic, the door blocks can be painted in playful colors.

Door of Secrets

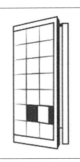

Several designs are built with purposeful storage included. This crafty yet hardy door does double duty with slide-out box compartments that allow storage. It's almost like a door full of drawers! It is astonishing how much can be hidden away in the cubby-holes of this door. Refer to our pinterest page for other similar designs.

Other Doors

Other door types include fire-rated doors to the garage, interior basement doors, and attic doors — which are not really doors at all.

Fire-Rated Door

Safety doors with fire-resistance ratings are required to be installed between the garage and the home. The purpose is to ensure that the door shuts automatically so that toxic fumes from the car won't seep into the house. Also the door is heavy, and offers tight weather stripping, which helps stop a fire from spreading. It is a passive type of fire protection system and required by the building codes, as home inspectors frequently point out in their reports.

Basement Door

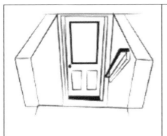

An interior basement door may be a regular-looking vertical door, or it may be a door in the floor. Either way, the purpose is to keep the basement area separate from the house. The door opens and leads to stairs going down into the basement, which may not be insulated. Therefore, the basement door should have heavy weather-stripping to keep the house energy efficient.

Attic Door

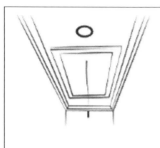

An attic hatch is a simple square opening in the ceiling. Some panels that can be lifted and scooted for attic access. Most doors are hinged and some even have retractable ladders that unfold and slide out. In California, attic hatches are often hidden inside closets. Livable attics may have a small hinged door in the wall, rather than the ceiling.

False Door

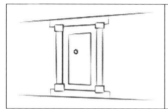

This type of door is not even a door at all! It's a decorative door panel that is installed directly on a wall to give the illusion of a doorway. It may be used to bring architectural style to a room.

Hidden Door

Remember watching mystery movies, and the house had a hidden lever that could open the creaky door to a secret room? Secret doors are often disguised as bookshelves and can hide another room, or a passageway to another part of the house. Also used to conceal valuable objects, or make more efficient use of space, it could be a wine door underneath the stairs!

Wood Types

Solid wood doors may be unfinished, pre-finished, or finished. Wood species used for doors includes:

- Asian Rosewood
- Bamboo
- Black Cherry
- Mahogany
- Maple
- Monkeywood
- Pecan Hickory

- Rubberwood
- Table Mountain Pine
- Taeng wood
- Teak or Golden Teak
- Walnut
- White Oak

Conclusion

Doors set the ambiance for a home; and exquisite doors may even sell a listing! As a real estate sales agent, we understand the importance of doors. We inspect doors as part of our walk-through. Secure doors ensure our listings are protected safely. And for our marketing ads, we learn how to describe unique door features that make our listings stand out.

Now that we know how to describe the exterior doors of our listings, we're confident that we can meet more sellers and get more listings. Because now you can identify every type of interior door correctly, and show your clients that you really care!

10. Walls

View sample illustrations on our pinterest board:

http://www.pinterest.com/realtyproadvisr/walls

What's the first thing a buyer sees when they drive up to view a home? The exterior walls! A home's walls define the character of the home, and can lend to the curb appeal that adds value to a home. Today's topic is all about walls: exterior, interior, and all sorts of others.

A wall is a flat, vertical structural component that is part of the building. Walls have 3 components: structure (the framework), finish surface, and insulation (between the structure and finish). Plumbing pipes and electrical wires are often inside the walls. Both exterior and interior

Exterior Walls

Exterior walls are weatherproof; they shield the sun, wind, and elements. They secure our home and protect us from outside threats. They define a house's boundaries and set the tone for the neighborhood. More importantly, they provide the structure of the house and support the weight of the roof and any upper stories.

Exterior Wall Materials

A system of strong, well-built walls is like an envelope that wraps around the home. It can keep pollutants and allergens at bay while improving energy efficiency. Walls are often built from local raw materials abundant in the region. The local climate often determines the standard building materials. Let's look at some popular building materials for walls.

Stucco

A thin layer of cement and sand sprayed on as the finish coat which then hardens, stucco is highly durable and resists weathering. Stucco is more fire-retardant than wood, that is why it's popular California and the West Coast. It lasts indefinitely and rarely requires maintenance. Stucco may have a hand-troweled finish for an upscale look.

Wood Beams

Wooden beams, such as 2x4s, are the most popular type of wall structures. The beams are assembled into a series of posts, nailed together, and secured to the concrete (or other) foundation. Beams are manufactured from timber, which of course attracts termites and deteriorates over time. Many builders now use specially treated wood to repel termites and ensure a longer lasting structure.

Brick & Mortar

Bricks, made from hardened clay, are popular on the East Coast and the Midwest. They are "glued" together with mortar (which dries into concrete material) and constructed in a staggered pattern to add strength. In areas prone to earthquakes, brick walls are viewed as unsafe because the mortar turns into "jelly" during earth movement, and an entire wall could collapse on its residents. Brick walls are enjoyed for their charm and character.

Cinder Blocks

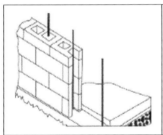

Cinder blocks are large bricks and each side is hollow in the middle. Rebar (metal bar) is threaded through the middles, and then reinforced by concrete. Cinder blocks may be the base of a wall, but will have a finish over the blocks. Also known as concrete blocks.

Metal Cladding

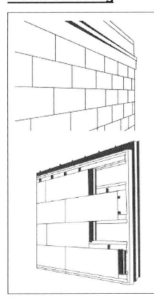

The finishing material of metal is often aluminum because it is lightweight shell, and yet resists the elements well. It is more durable than wood because it resists peeling, scratching, and flaking. Metal, even if treated, may rust over time. The most common application for metal cladding are the long overlapping panels seen on manufactured homes.

T1-11 Siding

Pronounced "tee-one-eleven", T1-11 is durable wood or plywood siding product popular during the 1970's.

Composite Siding

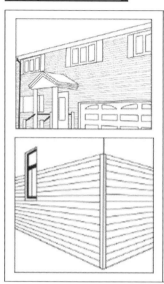

A composite material made of plastics, mineral fibers, or hard foam that is resilient and repels corrosion. Similar to the metal overlapping panels, it is convenient to cover a house, but is more durable than metal.

Wood Shingles

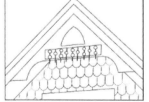

Wooden shingles are rarely used due to the fire hazard and eventual deterioration from sun and moisture exposure. May also be wood shakes or planks.

Logs

 Tree timbers, either factory-hewn or hand-stripped to preserve the wood pattern, are assembled in a lengthwise "peg" pattern. Many log homes are purchased in kits ready to build. Log homes are admired for their unique "mountain" architecture.

Stone / Brick / Rock Veneer

 Adding a stone finish to an exterior walls is more time-consuming than spraying stucco, but it adds immense character and is naturally weather-proof. Often stone cladding will be added to enhance the architectural qualities, and will only rise up 2 or 3 feet from the ground. A stone, brick, or rock veneer is a façade wall (for cosmetic effects only) constructed from thin slices of stone, rock, or brick. Stone materials include slate, marble, travertine, granite, or limestone.

Weatherboard / Wood Cladding

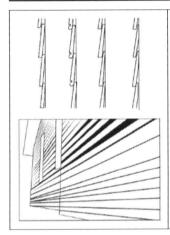 Weatherboard consists of wood strips places over each other in rows. It was used for many years as the staple of exterior siding, but requires continual maintenance to paint and seal the wood in an attempt to prevent deterioration. This material is also a haven for termites who destroy the wood.

Vinyl Cladding

 Exterior slats constructed from vinyl or plastic mimics wood, but is longer lasting and requires less maintenance.

Straw Bale

 Environmentally conscious home builders are starting to incorporate straw bale walls, which insulate a house extremely well. Straw is an alternative to traditional construction materials.

Adobe

 Adobe is mixed using clay, sand, and water. The adobe can then be applied directly to a wall, or hardened into "mud bricks". Because they are constructed from the earth, adobe walls help keep a house cool during hot summer months.

Cob

 Made from natural materials, cob is a mixture of sand, clay, dirt, straw, and water. It is comparable to adobe and revered for its fireproof properties. This eco-friendly wall is thick and rustic, and may be seen on a home in a rural area. It lasts for many years without maintenance, and insulates extremely well.

Other wall materials include Tile (clay or slate) and Fiber Cement (panels or planks).

Interior Walls

Interior walls separate rooms, offer privacy, and reduce noise. They define sections, add character, and allow artistic effects to shine through. Murals, mosaics, and other designs are popular artistic features that add warmth and ambiance to a home. Some interior walls also have a practical feature – they support the ceiling structure. They are usually insulated.

Interior Wall Types

The quality of a wall depends upon the construction materials, acoustic rating, and fire resistance level.

Partition Walls

Partition walls are constructed to separate rooms and are not load-bearing. They may be added or removed when renovating a house. For example, most interior bedroom walls are partition walls.

Portable Walls

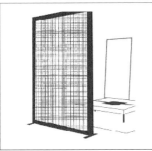

Room dividers and movable partitions are used to segment areas within a house, or open several smaller spaces to create one large room. They may be sliding on a track, have wheels, or fold away so they can be moved easily when needed. Partitions can be constructed of material stretched across a wooden frame, a stained glass door, decorative wrought iron, or panels of natural materials such as wicker.

Pony Walls

These are half-walls about 3 feet high, used to visually divide rooms while still keeping an open style and feel. A pony wall is a decorative feature and not a load-bearing wall. Also known as a stem wall.

Interior Wall Materials

Interior walls set the tone of a home and enhance the atmosphere. Their construction may include the following materials:

- Wood
- Green Board
- Concrete Sheeting
- Drywall / Sheet rock
- Plaster
- Venetian Plaster
- Tile
- Veneer

Interior Wall Visual Effects

Walls don't have to be boring! Just look at some of the many visual applications that add texture, light, and ambiance to a room:

- Paint
- Beadboard

- Mural
- Wallpaper
- Art Panels (such as 3-D)
- Patterns (created with patterned paint roller)
- Wainscoting
- Feature Walls
- Niches (to display art)
- Wood Paneling
- Fabric (applied with starch)
- Stenciled or painted designs
- Rustic wooden slats

Other items that are part of the interior wall construction include baseboard, molding, and bottom plates. Made from wood, resin, or medium density fiberboard (MDF), they add visual elegance and create an attractive finished look.

Other Walls

Load Bearing & Non-Load-Bearing Walls

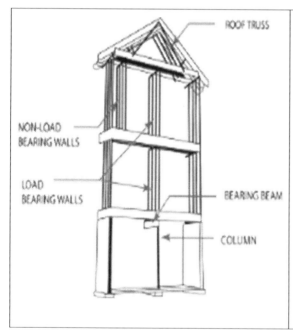

Load Bearing Walls

They support the roof, ceiling, and structural weigh of the house. All exterior walls are load-bearing, and some interior walls are also. Load bearing walls are aligned with the support beams. These walls cannot be removed without risk of the ceiling collapsing. AKA Bearing Wall.

Non-Load-Bearing Walls

These interior walls do not support the house's weight, as their main purpose is to divide room (partition walls). They usually run perpendicular to floor and ceiling joists, and can be moved (after any plumbing or electrical within the walls are relocated).

Systems-Built Walls

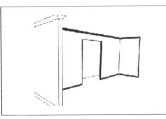	Manufactured in factories, systems-built walls are custom constructed or fashioned after a template. Laws for pre-fabricated walls are more stringent, therefore they may be more robust than typical stick-built walls.

Shared / Common Walls

	Interior walls that separate adjoining homes, wherein each resident's home has one side of the wall. This is common in condos and apartments. Where an HOA is involved, read the rules carefully to determine who is responsible for plumbing leaks in common walls. AKA "Party Walls".

Conclusion

Now that you know all about walls, don't keep this knowledge in a box! Educate your buyers and satisfy your sellers. Let your skills and experience shine through.

11. Stairs

View sample illustrations on our pinterest board:

http://www.pinterest.com/realtyproadvisr/stairs

Picture a gracious lady in a stunning evening gown slowly descending a magnificent staircase, pausing for effect at just the right moment. Wouldn't you agree that a luxurious winding staircase broadening to a grand foyer can lend ambiance to your listing. Buyers crave the look that evokes a classic Hollywood movie scene unfolding in their new home.

Does your new listing boast the "stairway to heaven"? How do you highlight in your advertisements? Stairs are classified by their path and direction. In today's topic, we show you 4 types of staircase flights: straight, landing turns, curving, and winder. We discuss various staircase era styles along with some of the noteworthy stair features you may encounter while showing property. In showing homes to buyers, feng shui fans may insist that stairs cannot be facing the front doorway.

Straight Flight Stairs

The most functional set of stairs is one that offers a straight path between levels. Each tread is built in a straight line from entrance to exit of the staircase without turns. Typically, 16 is the maximum number of treads between floors.

No Landing

A straight staircase with no landing simply goes from top to bottom with treads (steps) each the same height, size, and distance. This most basic type of staircase is often seen in residential houses because it's the simplest and least expensive to build.

Intermediate Landing

When the straight staircase pauses in the middle of the stairs with a landing platform, that is known as an intermediate landing. By dividing the flight of stairs, it makes the climb easier for people who may need to pause and catch their breath. Inserting a landing absorbs more space from the floor plan, however.

Compact Stairs (Goose Steps / Sambo Stairs)

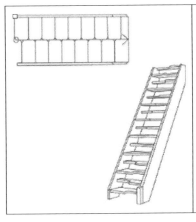

When space is extremely limited, the builder may construct a shorter staircase made with "goose" steps, wherein the tread is larger on one side than the other. The steps alternate with the large part of the step being on the right, then left, then right again. Compact staircases may be seen in basements, utility rooms, or areas infrequently accessed. People must be careful to place each foot on the correct step for the sake of safety to avoid the hazard of falling.

Pulldown (Attic Ladder)

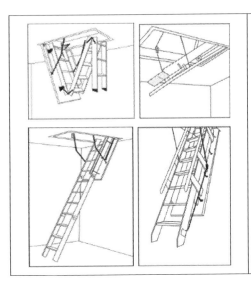

An attic hatch opens to reveal a complete staircase hidden in the ceiling. The 2 types of attic access stairs are: fold-up ladders (accordion style fold) and slide-out ladders (telescoping style). The treads are narrow and caution should be exercised, just as when climbing a ladder.

Landing Turn Stairs

Straight stairs with a landing that turn the direction of the stairs are known as landing turn stairs. They can rotate the stairway by a quarter, a double, or a half turn.

Quarter Landing Stairs (L Shaped)

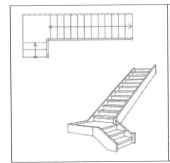

Stairs with a quarter landing have a platform half way up, and form an "L" shape as they make the 90 degree corner turn. The landing is typically a square shaped platform.

Double Quarter Landing (Double L)

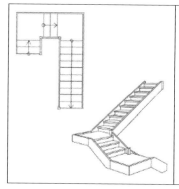

Similar to a quarter landing, a double landing staircase has 2 landings, each with a 90 degree corner turn. Together, they make a 180 turn, but with stairs in between the 2 landings.

Half Landing Stairs (U Shaped)

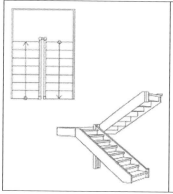

A staircase that make a 180 degree U-shaped turn is known as a half landing staircase because it makes a half turn. The 2 half-flights of stairs run parallel to each other. The landing platform is typically larger than a quarter landing because people must make 2 turns. It's easier to walk up the flight of stairs with a pause in the middle.

Curving Stairs

A curving staircase curls in a circle or an arc pattern, either gently or sharply. The three types are arched, curved, or spiral staircases.

Arched Stairs

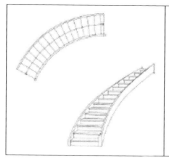

Arched stairways curve gently as they rise in one direction. Each step (tread) is wider on the outside of the arch and narrower on the inside; therefore each step is a slight trapezoid wedge shape. These graceful and luxurious staircases are crafted with custom workmanship. Think "Gone With the Wind" era.

Curved

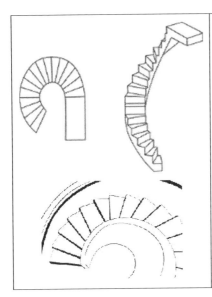

Curved staircases twist around in a full circle. Each tread is trapezoid shaped so they are not as easy to walk up or down as a straight staircase. Either modern or sophisticated home styles bode well to curved stairs.

Spiral Stairs

Staircases that wrap sharp circles around a vertical beam are known as spiral. They are the most difficult type to maneuver because of the pie-shaped treads (steps) and are generally reserved for tight spaces or when the stairs will not be accessed frequently. Most are welded from steel metal. Spiral circular stairs are built attached to a central pole in the middle and commonly seen in lofts.

Winder Stairs

Winder stairs turn at a 90 degree or 180 degree angle around corners but do not have a landing platform. Therefore, the steps that turn corners are trapezoid shaped — wider on the outside and narrow on the inside. It occupies less floor space than staircases with landings. They boast graceful, fluid styles, as compared to the square look of landing staircases. Because of each tread's unique size, winder stairs are more difficult to design and more expensive to build.

Single Winder Stairs

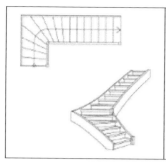 Single winders are staircases that make a 90 degree right angle turn (quarter turn) without a landing. In other words, the stairs go around the corner following the same pattern with treads at approximately the same intervals.

Double Winder Stairs

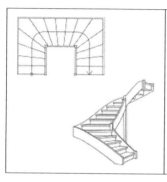 Double winders are similar to single winders, except that they turn by 180 degrees in a half circle. This half turn may also be achieved by building 2 quarter turns (90 degrees each). Larger treads are easier to climb but take up more space.

Era Styles

Various period styles include traditional, modern, classic, contemporary, and feature stairs. The design style often reflects the architectural character of the house when it was built.

Traditional

 Staircases that reflect an old-fashioned era in which a house was built are referred to as traditional. They capture the house's essence and the period in which it was constructed.

Modern

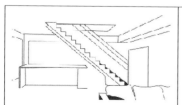 Clean and sleek, the minimalist style is best known as modern. It has simple lines and neutral colors.

Classic

The elegant look of a classic style stairway imparts a formal mood to the house. Intricate details such as custom carved wood echo the creative flair of the past.

Contemporary

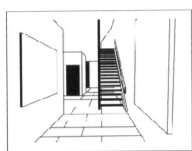

Bold and outstanding, a contemporary staircase radiates a confident vibe into the house. Its breathtaking design draws attention.

Feature

A feature staircase makes the home's distinctive interior stand out because visitors recognize the exceptional architecture instantly. Its one-of-a-kind style blends artistic design in a unique way and dominates the home's entrance.

Staircase Construction

The following terms define stair pieces and parts you may need to reference in your daily real estate business.

Baserail

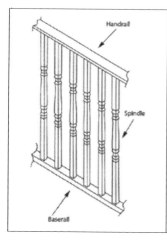

The baserail is the bottom horizontal plank of the handrail. The spindles sit on top of it and form the base of the railing.

Bullnose Step

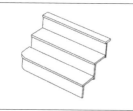

Bullnose steps project horizontally from the top of each step, jutting out over the top of each riser.

Cap

Similar to a finial, a cap is a wooden square placed at the top of the main posts on the handrail. Its purpose is decorative.

Finial (Newel Cap)

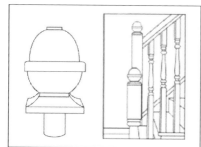

A finial is a decorative ornament at the top of the main posts on the handrail. They are typically a similar design to match the spindles, either wood or metal.

Freestanding

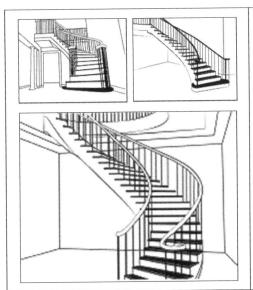

A freestanding staircase is open underneath. It is not supported by walls, or built on top of a structure. The purpose of the design concept is to convey a modern, elegant look.

Handrail (Guardrail)

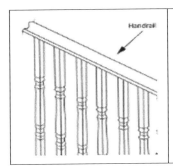

The handrail is used as a guide for people to hold onto when ascending or descending the stairs. It is a safety feature. The handrail is supported by spindles.

Landing

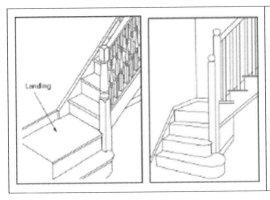

A landing is a large, open platform either within the staircase, or at the top/bottom. Landings within the flight of stairs are a resting place for the stair climber, or allow the steps to change direction.

Open Risers

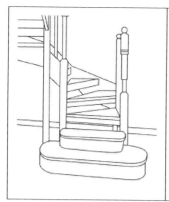

On a freestanding staircase, when the risers of each step are non-existent they are called open risers. There is an open space between each stair. Builders use open risers to create a spacious, airy design feature.

Pie Stairs (Kite Stairs)

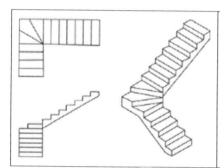

The 2 or 3 large triangular-shaped treads that round a corner in lieu of a landing are called pie or kite stairs. They are built when there is not enough room for a landing to turn the corner. Pie stairs can be dangerous to climb if people are not careful to watch their footing.

Riser

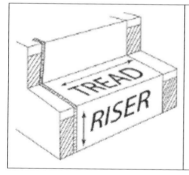

A piece of wood inserted vertically between each step, known as the face.

Spindle (Baluster)

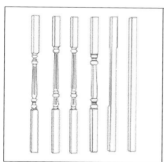

The vertical rods, usually wood or metal, that connect the baserail at the bottom of the sides to the handrail.

Stairwell

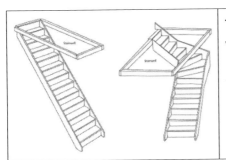

The stairwell is the space left open by the builder in which the stairs are inserted. It refers to the "footprint" encompassed by the stairs. Generally, staircase spaces and voids are calculated as living space within the house.

Step

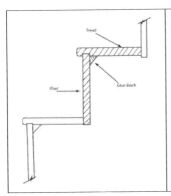

A step refers to both the tread (horizontal wood surface) and the riser (vertical wood surface between the treads).

Stringer

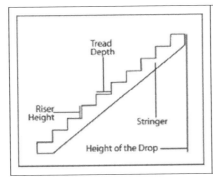

The stringer is the diagonal line that runs up the length and height of the staircase.

Tread

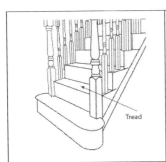

The top of each step on which people place their feet is called the tread. It is a horizontal surface, usually built from wood.

Wall Rail

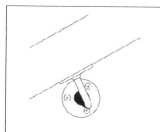

When a handrail is attached to the wall with brackets rather than sitting on top of spindles, it is referred to as a wall rail.

Under-Stair Storage

Surprise storage, or even a children's play house, may be tucked away under the stairs. Some under-stair areas enclose a guest bathroom. Imaginative designers use the space between treads as a bookcases, or the back of a freestanding staircase for shelving. The most clever concept, however, is when each stair actually contains a pull-out drawer for storage!

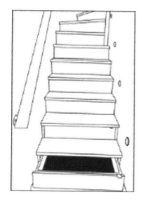

Conclusion

In an art deco style house, you may see unusual staircases such as floating stairs (attached to the wall on only 1 side) or suspended staircases (hanging from above). Last but not least, you may come across emergency escape stairs in a multi-level stair format (usually on the houses' exterior). But no matter what house you list for sale, or what home you view with your buyer clients, you now have the confidence to describe every type of stairway you encounter in your real estate career.

12. Flooring

View sample illustrations on our pinterest board:

http://www.pinterest.com/realtyproadvisr/floors

When you walk into a home with a prospective buyer, their eyes are often drawn up and they never notice the floor — unless it's exceptional. But wouldn't you agree that whether fabulous or lackluster, flooring sets the tone for a house's interior design. Subliminally, the floor can make or break a buyer's first showing.

The floor is the basic building frame of a home and insulates from the ground or the story underneath. It provides a comfortable surface for residents to walk upon, as well as aesthetic value. Whether hardwood planks or wall-to-wall carpet, floor coverings can provide a décor base that compliments the ambiance.

In today's topic we will explore the primary types of residential flooring: wood and natural materials, laminate and reconstructed wood, vinyl, carpet, and others. Plus, find out about trends and hacks for eco-conscious flooring. (Tile flooring is covered in the next chapter.)

Planks

Whether the house boasts handsome solid wood, durable engineered hardwood, or wood-look laminate, good installation is the key to longevity. Professional installation ensures wood flooring will stay in good condition for many years. Homeowners can expect the flooring to adjust to the house, expanding and contracting after installation.

Solid Wood

Character and charm exude from original solid wood floors hand-crafted from local timber a century ago. Admired for their natural beauty, solid woods are tough and resilient. Many an older home's original wood floors are discovered in near-perfect condition after being covered with carpet for many years. Even those floors with nicks, scratches, and dents are showcased as "distressed" flooring.

Wood flooring is usually installed on top of a plywood sub-floor or concrete foundation, but in some houses the wood flooring was the foundation also. Planks are created from solid pieces of wood, milled to either a narrow or wide board size. Wide board planks create a clean, modern look while narrow planks reflect a more traditional, historic elegance.

A wood floor can enhance a house significantly and reward the sellers with a higher sales price depending on the timber species, the plank thickness, and the finish craftsmanship quality. Home owners enjoy wood floors because they are known to be hypoallergenic and simple to clean. The National Wood Flooring Association (NWFA) conducted a flooring study and discovered that 96% of interior designers consider wood floors one of their best options for matching a variety of design styles professionally.

Downsides include the cost, which can be expensive, and the expanding/contracting function of natural wood depending on the weather and humidity. Because wood is porous and absorbs water, they are not installed in kitchens, bathrooms, or basements. Wood floors are subject to water damage such as mold and termites, unless treated and maintained. Buyers inspecting a home for purchase may want to check hardwood floors for squeaks, buckling, and fading / discoloration.

Parquet wood flooring is formed with patterned blocks or strips of wood, and perhaps wood or other material inlays. Parquet is usually laid in squares rather than planks.

Wood Types

Popular solid woods include native species such as maple, pine, ash, walnut, and oak. Imported timber from acacia and teak trees have spawned a hue of colors and wood flairs. Varieties such as black walnut, hickory pecan, mahogany, and bubinga (African rosewood) have gained popularity. Exquisite Ipe hardwood and rare timber from Belize are now highly desirable for flooring.

Surface Finish Options

Depending on how the edges are finished, the seam joints can create a stylish look for the flooring.

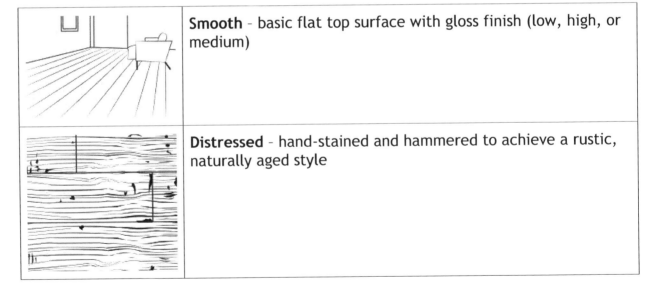

	Smooth – basic flat top surface with gloss finish (low, high, or medium)
	Distressed – hand-stained and hammered to achieve a rustic, naturally aged style

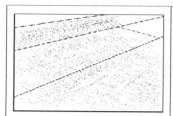	**Hand Scraped** – appears to be hand-milled with a pocket knife
	Stained – shades of color can impart light hues or dark tones

Wood planks can be finished either before or after installing. Most hardwood flooring kits are pre-finished at the factory rather than finished on site.

	**Pre-Finished Solid** - Planks are sanded, stained, and finished with urethane when they arrive from the factory, ready to install. The installation is quicker and easier.
	**Site-Finished Solid** - For custom flooring, staining unfinished planks onsite is the solution. Sanding at the job site means uneven floors will be completely smooth across the entire surface. Colors and stains can be personalized to match other household flooring.

Janka Hardness Test

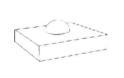	Harder woods stand up to foot traffic better and resist wear and tear from furniture, children, and pets. On the other hand, harder wood is difficult to saw through. Janka Hardness scale rates a wood's hardness between 0 and 4,000 points. A higher number means a harder wood, but not necessarily more expensive pricing (wood cost is based on species availability). Appearance and life length are also determined by traffic and maintenance.

Douglas Fir is one of the softest woods at 660 points, which means it dents and scratches easily so it may need to be repaired or replaced sooner. American Cherry, a soft wood, ranks 950, whereas Brazilian Cherry tops the chart at 2,820 points. White and Red Oaks garnered middle rankings. Note: hardness is not equivalent to strength or foot comfort.

Installation

Conventional wood flooring is designed with the tongue-and-groove assembly. The sides click into place and create a "floating" floor because it's not affixed to the foundation. But, for additional strength, the planks can also be nailed into the foundation using blind nailing (which hides the nails driven in from an angle). Wood floors should be installed with a sub-floor protective mat between the foundation and finished flooring.

Care and Maintenance

The life of a hardwood floor can be extended by preventing wear and tear and protecting high traffic areas. For example: carpet runners in hallways, felt pads on furniture legs, de-clawing pets, and removing shoes in the house (especially high heels or spiked shoes). Sweeping regularly helps to prevent sand from scraping the glossy finish, and mopping up water spills immediately will reduce staining.

Engineered Hardwood

Wood floors expand with heat and contract with cold weather — so for basements or houses in extreme climates, engineered hardwood is the perfect solution. Several sheets of different types of wood are laminated on top of each other to form cross-ply strength.

Engineered hardwood floors are preferred on top of concrete slab foundations. Solid wood floors perform best in homes on a raised foundation. But homes built on concrete, or below grade (basements), perform best with engineered hardwood.

Engineered floors are installed by floating over a sub-floor or by nailing, stapling, or gluing down. Compared to hardwood, it costs slightly less and installation is quicker. Because of the resins and adhesives, planks will off-gas over time. Home owners appreciate that engineered flooring planks can be sanded and refinished (minimally), just like regular wood.

Laminate

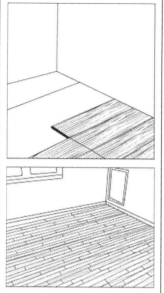

Is it real wood or is it laminate? With modern manufacturing, it can be difficult to distinguish! "Faux wood" laminate planks simulate a natural wood look and are an affordable alternative for homeowners. To achieve a realistic look, laminate planks are embossed with HD photos of wood planks. Laminate is durable, resistant to rotting, and low maintenance. It doesn't fade or dent, and it holds up to weather changes better than solid wood.

However, laminate is sensitive to water (moisture will bloat the edges) and deep scratches cannot be sanded out. With a floating floor, removing and replacing a plank is a difficult and tedious process. Pergo is a popular name brand of laminate flooring.

Composition

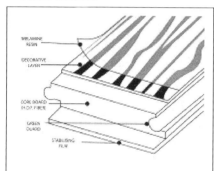

Produced with natural, recycled, and synthetic materials, the core is covered with a decorative applique that mimics wood or stone. Laminate planks are manufactured with layers of material bonded together with resin, pressure, and heat.

Products vary by brand, most consisting of 4 or 5 layers:

- Top layer 1: Clear overlay of melamine or cellulose that protects against minor surface wear and imparts sheen
- Top layer 2: Decorative wood-look high res photo
- Middle layer 3: HDF (High Density Fiberboard) core made from wood composite which uses all parts of the tree
- Bottom layer 4: Moisture barrier to resist water and vapors
- Bottom layer 5: Balancing film for dimensional stability

Surface Texture

Because laminate floors imitate natural wood, sophisticated modern technology copy timber in both the look of wood grain and the texture. A few replica textures in laminate include:

	**Smooth** – flat, even surface with gloss finish (low, high, or medium)
	**Embossed (Textured)** – wood grain grooves rise out of the surface giving a slight 3D effect
	**Embossed in Registration** – accurate reproduction of the natural grain grooves
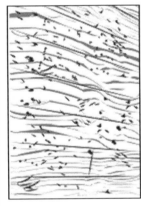	**Distressed** – appears antique and used (a hot trend in real wood floors)
	**Hand Scraped** – another new trend is wood that looks as if it was hand-crafted, where long bumps stick up out of the surface

Edge Seams

Each plank has a slight cut on the edges, which create the following seams.

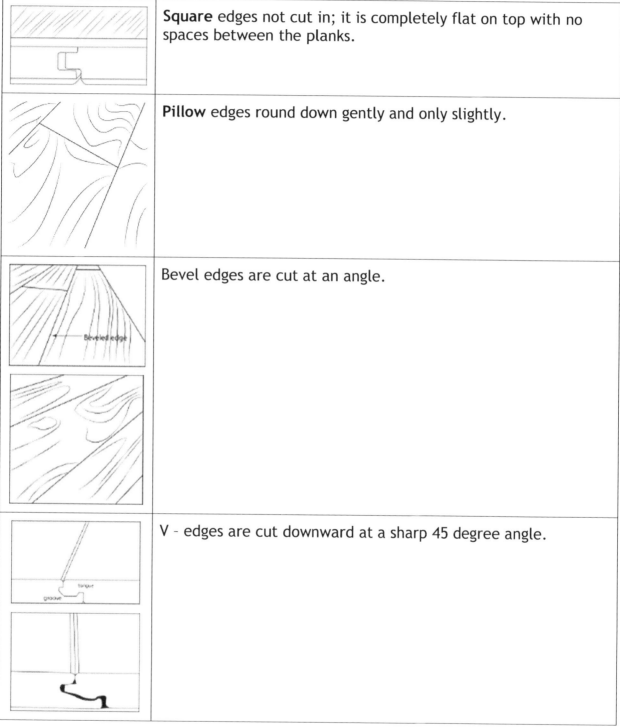

	Square edges not cut in; it is completely flat on top with no spaces between the planks.
	Pillow edges round down gently and only slightly.
	Bevel edges are cut at an angle.
	V – edges are cut downward at a sharp 45 degree angle.

AC Rating

Laminate flooring durability is rated based on an AC (Abrasion Class) scale. It should be able to resist stress and withstand the foot traffic of a house. Flooring with higher AC rating is typically more expensive.

- AC1 = Moderate Residential (best for low traffic areas like closets & bedrooms)
- AC2 = General Residential (moderate traffic such as a dining / living rooms)
- AC3 = Heavy Residential (high traffic rooms such as kitchens and hallways)
- AC4 and AC5 are for commercial buildings.

Installation

Laminate flooring "floating floor" planks are installed by snapping the pieces together with the grooves in the middle of each panel. Referred to as a "click in" system or a "glueless click", most laminate flooring is floating. This installation is preferred because as the foundation of a house shifts, the flooring doesn't break apart. Other installation types include glued joints and pre-glued — the seams are stronger but installation is more extensive. Laminate is installed with a vinyl mat underlay.

Natural Materials

Bamboo

Although bamboo plank flooring looks and functions just like wood plank flooring, there's a huge difference: bamboo is a grass, not a timber. Grass is sustainable because it naturally re-grows new shoots after harvesting. Mature bamboo can be harvested in only 6 years (compared to hardwood trees that take 60 - 80 years). Even though it's a grass, bamboo is actually harder than wood — up to 25% tougher than oak! And strand (compressed) bamboo is even more durable.

Similar to wood, bamboo floor surface variations can include distressed, hand-scraped, and antique look. This eco-friendly flooring can be installed using tongue and groove or click-lock assembly. It may be a bit more costly than wood, but lasts longer.

Cork

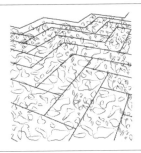

Think of cork bulletin boards, then imagine how cushiony that would feel underfoot. Cork floors are collected naturally from trees, but unlike bulletin boards they are durable and spill-resistant. Homeowners can select from a variety of colors and designs much more elegant than bulletin boards.

Residents enjoy the comfortable "give" of cork flooring. It's also practical because it insulates heat and provides a sound barrier. Environmentally conscious homeowners clamor for cork because it is harvested by peeling away the bark layer while keeping the tree intact.

Man-Made Materials

Concrete

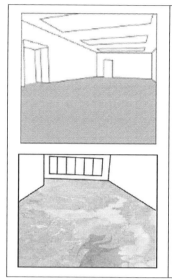

Considered a man-made material, concrete is actually produced from rocks and other natural sources. A dry mix consisting of aggregate (sand, ground-up rocks, and/or gravel) is combined with water and a cement paste that hardens into a thick, solid, indestructible surface. Most often seen in driveways, patios, and garages, concrete is becoming a popular flooring for basements, main living spaces, and busy household thoroughfares such as hallways. When the house foundation is a concrete slab, home owners desiring a concrete floor merely need to remove the flooring and use the foundation as a floor. Low maintenance and ease of cleaning are a plus with polished floors.

Usually built with rebar reinforcements to add flexibility, concrete is porous so it needs to be sealed with an overlay finish — urethane or acrylic are common. Colorful surface applications include: paint, stain, acid stain, and epoxy topcoat. Concrete can also be dyed before pouring it. Striking designs can be created by scoring patterns and varying borders, colors, stains, and finishes. Faux wood or ceramic tile patterns on concrete can look realistic and give "contemporary" a new meaning.

Rubber

Yes, rubber is not just for tires — Europeans have been installing rubber floors for years. From square tiles for the garage or basement, to puzzle-shaped pieces for a playroom or studio, to soft rolls for the office or workout room, rubber flooring has a variety of layouts. Liquid latex is tapped from rubber trees, and then refined. Rubber floors in a main living area give an industrial look that's intriguing yet sensible — it is low maintenance, non-slip, and long-lasting. Most importantly, it's indulgent for the feet. Consumers who install re-ground rubber (post industrial recycled materials) help the environment too! Foam rubber is another softer variation, AKA "foam".

3-D Murals

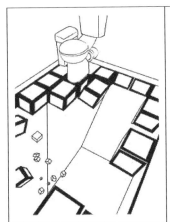

For a mind-blowing dramatic effect, floors capture attention with realistic (and sometimes scary) 3-D murals. Puzzle tiles and self-leveling floors are the base for spectacular designs in bathrooms, kids' rooms, and even main living areas. Real-life photos are printed extra large, glued to a concrete floor, covered with epoxy, and finished with a protective lacquer coat.

For a novel approach to flooring, check out the artistic paint designs that feel like walking on water and other optical illusions as shown on our pinterest page.

Carpet

Carpet adds texture, warmth, and hues to a home. Thick carpet, along with dense padding, provide sound-proofing and energy efficiency. It's soft and cushiony for the feet and covers imperfections in the floor foundation. On the other hand, carpet collects dander and dust, leading to allergies and asthma. Deep vacuuming is required to remove the dirt attracted from shoes, and when moist it may harbor mildew.

Carpet from a roll is quick to install, and less expensive than other flooring types. Wall-to-wall carpet is easily installed across tack strips glued to the edges of the floor (along the bottom of each wall) for permanent and complete room coverage.

Berber carpet, cherished for its low loop pile, were originally hand-woven by North African Berber tribe using hand-spun knots. They are known to be inexpensive and durable, but a pulled-up yard can "run", pulling up an entire line across the carpet.

Area rugs, often made from carpet, are small rectangles or circles placed on top of flooring, and used for design accents or catching dirt in high traffic areas. Rugs are personal possessions, whereas carpets are attached to the real property.

Loops and Piles

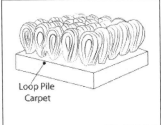

Loop Pile Carpet

Carpet is created when yard strands are sewn into a backing, producing loops. The loops form a "loop" carpet. Loops with varied heights produce a "patterned loop" carpet. Cutting the yarn loops on top creates a "cut pile" (AKA texture or plush). Loops and cuts can even be combined to fashion a sophisticated pattern.

Padding

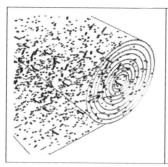

A roll of padding is installed on top of the foundation, underneath the carpet layer. Pads are graded by thickness, quality, and material composition. The biggest challenge with pads is that once they are wet (from carpet spills) they can mildew. Once deteriorated, the pads must be replaced.

Tack Strips

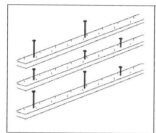

Long, thin wood strips lined with carpet tacks are installed along the edges of the floor. The tacks face upward to grab and keep the carpet in place. Tack strips are installed by nailing and gluing onto the foundation. Fastened leaving a small gap between the wall, they allow wall-to-wall carpet have a neat, finished look once installed.

Floor Components

Sub-Floors

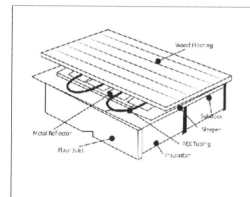

A sub-floor is an underlying material that protects the flooring. They also reduce noise and provide heat/cold insulation. Some sub-floors provide a layer of cushioning too. To shield the home further, a plywood sub-floor can be nailed over the foundation, and then the underlayment material secured on top. Sub-floor types include poly membrane, foam underlayment, foil advanced underlayment, DRIcore®, cement backer board, and cork.

A membrane is an underlayment sheet of material that protects both foundation and flooring. It prevents moisture damage from leaking through either way. Polyethylene uncoupling membrane is a flexible rubberized rolled sheet with small square grids or round pockets. It provides a stable base for tile, and prevents cracking by minimizing movement.

Foam Underlayment for Laminate Flooring preps the surface with a roll of foam matting. Soundbloc is a popular brand for builders.

Advanced Flooring Underlayment from FloorComfort is a mat encased in thermos foil that unrolls or unfolds for installation under laminate floors. It smooths the foundation surface and preps for leveled laminate installation.

DRIcore® is a moisture barrier for basement concrete foundations that allows concrete to breathe while protecting the flooring. Banish cold, damp concrete floors and the mildew that breeds in humid basements with sub-floors under the flooring.

Cement backer board is used for tile in bathrooms; HardieBacker is a popular recognizable brand. Backer board is specially designed for moisture resistance in wet areas.

Natural sub-floor option cork insulates against noise and weather. This environmentally friendly material can underlay hardwood, laminate, or tile.

Radiant Heat

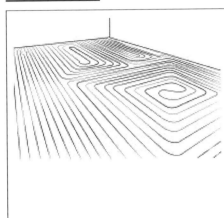

During the winter, heating systems are ideal under floors for cozy feet on cold mornings. Electric radiant coil mats, or hydronic systems (tubes for heated water), are installed on top of the foundation. Flat flooring, such as wood planks or tile, is laid on top. In-floor radiant heat systems are known to be robust and dependable. Since heat rises to the top of a room, home owners save energy costs by reducing furnace usage. Although expensive, heated floors are quiet and reduce air pollution compared to a forced-air system.

Floor Register

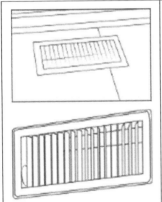

A metal vent cover in the floor that connects with the house's forced air vent system to pull in fresh air, or exhaust heated air. Rectangular or square-shaped registers often have "fins" that open or close the vent. They can be custom painted to match floor colors.

Sheeting

Vinyl

 Wide vinyl sheets of flooring are produced in rolls, ready for quick installation. Vinyl is an artificial material made from plasticizers and polyvinyl chloride, with color pigments. Because it resists water, vinyl is most effectively used in rooms with water — the kitchen, bathrooms, and laundry room. With low cost and quick installation, it is the least expensive flooring type. On the other hand, vinyl often scuffs or tears when appliances are moved across it — and it can't be restored completely.

When renovating houses it's typical to find several layers of vinyl flooring laid on top of each other because new layers can easily be installed on top of old layers. Vinyl may also be installed with self-stick adhesive tile squares so it's easier to replace damaged pieces — the downside is the seams are prone to water damage. Vinyl floors have more "give" than tile so they are ideal for children's playrooms.

Inlaid vinyl is thick and durable because it has a "wear layer" on top of inlaid color chips with a felt backing. Printed vinyl is less expensive because the paper-printed top coat only has a thin vinyl sheet underneath.

Linoleum

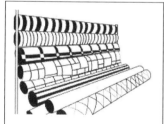 Remember those 1950's homes with industrial-looking linoleum floors? High quality inlaid linoleum floors can last for decades. The original linoleum flooring was manufactured from natural products, primarily linseed oil, with the addition of pine rosin, wood flour, cork dust, and mineral fillers. Unlike vinyl flooring, the color goes all the way through the linoleum because the color pigment is in the material.

Polyvinyl chloride floors are often referred to as "linoleum". They are flexible and long-lasting, and newer flooring is brighter colored and also fire-retardant. Some avoid it because they consider the toxic manufacturing materials harmful. They prefer the original non-allergenic linoleum produced from organic materials.

Baseboard

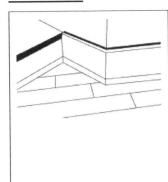

Trim, or molding, installed against the wall and rests along the edge of the floor. It provides an airtight envelope for the house, but its main function is aesthetic value. Baseboard can be made from wood or vinyl. It may match (or contrast) with the floor color and walls. "Baseboard covers the expansion gap next to the wall, which allows contraction and expansion of wood flooring," states Chamberlain. Lastly, baseboard gives the décor a finished look while hiding corner gaps and imperfections.

Conclusion

With your advanced knowledge of flooring options, you can shine as a buyer's agent. You know what a buyer may discover when they peek under the corner of a house listed for sale. Now you can advise your sellers about their flooring, enter it in the MLS correctly, and create an attractive ad to get your listing sold quickly.

13. Tile

View sample illustrations on our pinterest board:

http://www.pinterest.com/realtyproadvisr/tiles

Hooray! You just listed a luxury home for sale. But it includes 5 different types of tile on the floors, counters, shower wall, backsplash, and fireplace. How do you determine each style so you can showcase your new listing?

Later, you're out viewing homes with buyers and they notice cracked tile and decaying grout. How do you recognize and identify construction issues so you can explain them to your buyers?

Look for vibrant colors, interesting styles, and unique tile around the house. Thin glass tile in a green and gold design is perfectly eye-catching for a bathroom; bronze or copper tiles make astonishing kitchen backsplashes.

Popular in Mediterranean architecture, authentic tile floors bring a classic look to Spanish-style homes. Fireplaces tiled with stone are elegant and timeless. Marble flooring is an indication of luxurious indulgence. Tile can date a house when it reflects specific eras. For example: kitchen counters tiled with pink squares were popular in the 1950's, and the small hexagon black and white tile on the bathroom floor is a definitive 1930's look.

This chapter is a primer on tile types, materials, and patterns. We'll also give a brief tour of tile installation, because poor installation is the basis for tile problems that you may encounter while selling homes.

What is Tile?

Tiles are similar-sized pieces of flat, hardened clay that are permanently installed onto a floor or other surface. They are manufactured in thin squares (or other geometric shapes) and installed in a pattern with grout in between the tiles. Besides the ever-popular clay or ceramic, other tile materials include porcelain, quarried stone, manufactured metal, cement fiberboard, and formed or recycled glass.

Just to clear the confusion, "tiling" and "to tile" are verbs that refer to the processing of installing tile onto a surface. "Tiled" is an adjective that refers to a surface onto which tile was installed. The term "tile" may also refer to a building material applied in squares, such as carpet tiles which are squares of carpet installed individually. Rubber tiles can be effective garage flooring.

Advantages

Besides aesthetic beauty of the materials, colors, and patterns, tile is preferred for its clean-up ease. It is strong and durable in heavy-traffic areas. One huge advantage is that broken tiles can be removed and replaced, which cannot be done with vinyl. And in a warm climate, tile floors keep a house cooler.

Drawbacks

As a hard surface, tile is difficult to stand on continuously. Installation is permanent which means that removal is difficult. Tile can be mis-installed which causes problems for homeowners; and grout risks decay from mildew due to water intrusion. Porous tile, such as marble and stone, needs to be polished and sealed periodically.

Surface Durability Ratings

When buyers select a home, they should ensure that the surface durability of tile matches the intended usage. Can the entry way endure wear and tear from guests, children, and pets? Is the kitchen tile floor tough enough to withstand heavy traffic?

The PEI (Porcelain Enamel Institute) rates the surface durability of tile with the following 5 categories that apply to residential usage, classified as follows:

I.   Wall installation only, not suitable for floors
II. Floors with light traffic
III. Floors with moderate traffic, but no heavy objects (such as a car in a garage)
IV. Floors with heavy traffic
V.   Floors with very heavy traffic

Other measurements of quality besides the PEI ratings include: moisture absorption, tile density, and Mohs scale (mineral hardness and scratch resistance). Tile with a texture or a raised pattern has a higher COF (Coefficient of Friction), which means it is less slippery in wet areas. Consult your tile store vendor for more information.

Tile Types & Styles

The splendor of tile is that it can be installed in a plethora of patterns using basic materials in surprisingly simple shapes. A wide assortment of tile colors and textures lend to the artistic beauty of tile floors, walls, and counters.

Materials

Tile can be made from the following materials:

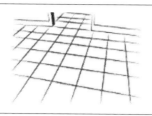	**Clay** – great for outdoors: walkway, front entry, and patio • Terracotta (an orange-brown clay) • Saltillo tile (popular Mexican tile good for indoor/outdoor use)
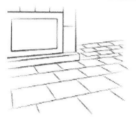	**Ceramic** – used indoors and often have a slick, shiny (glazed) surface. Popular for kitchen counters & backsplashes because they can withstand heat. • Glazed ceramic tile can be finished glossy, matte, or semi-glossy • Subway tiles are classic white ceramic brick-shaped tiles
	**Porcelain** – made from 50% clay and 50% white "feldspar" sand. More expensive but more durable than ceramic.
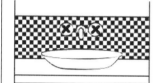	**Glass** – can be made from recycled materials. Mostly decorative, such as a backsplash or accent wall. Can be mixed with stone or ceramic tiles.
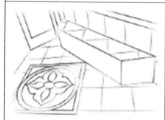	**Natural Stone** - quarried from mines and cut from slabs. Porous, but can be polished and sealed. Every tile is unique due to the patterns of nature. Textured tiles are ideal for wet floors such as bathrooms. Natural stone materials include: • Limestone • Travertine (from limestone) • Marble • Granite • Slate
	**Metal** – copper, bronze, pewter, tin, or other metals can be manufactured into thin tiles. Ideal for backsplashes or small accent walls.

Sizes & Shapes

Some basic sizes and shapes of tile include:

- Squares (8", 12", and 16" are common)
- Rectangles (oblong) (4" x 6" and 12" x 18" are typical)
- Long / thin rectangles (4" x 8" and 2" x 10" are typical)
- Ovals (very small; used for accents)
- Hexagons (6 sides) (1" is common)
- Octagons (8 sides) (1" is common)

Often, 2 or more sizes, shapes, and colors are combined to create a layout pattern, as shown below.

Patterns of Layout

Refer to our illustrations to get a bird's-eye view of the following popular patterns.

Straight Box Grid

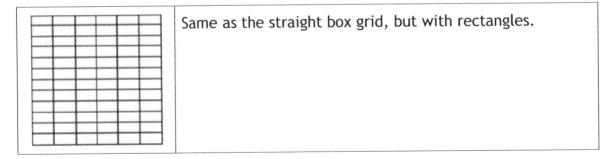

| | (AKA "Straight Lay" or "Simple Grid") – squares are lined up at the seams, installed in rows parallel to the walls, resulting in a plain box pattern. |

Straight Rectangle Grid

| | Same as the straight box grid, but with rectangles. |

Checkerboard

Alternating 2 different colors on every other square, with no same colors adjoining. Think: the classic old-fashioned 50's style black-and-white soda fountain store.

Waffle

A checkerboard pattern, with one of the two colored tiles consisting of several textured tiles as one.

Diagonal

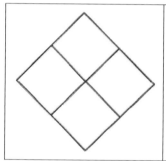

(AKA "Diamond") – same as the straight lay, except that tiles are tilted at a 45° degree angle in a diagonal pattern. The look is a bit classier than the straight box grid.

Diamond

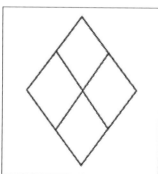

Diagonal pattern with diamond-shaped tiles.

Dotted Diagonal

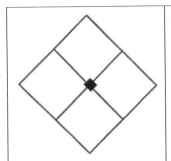

Same as the diagonal pattern, except that tiny accent tiles are inserted at every other corner. It really elevates the design of the diagonal style.

Alternating

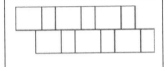

Square tiles alternated with rectangle tiles half the size of the squares. "Alternating Centered" pattern is a variation.

Running Bond

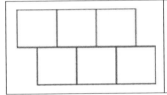

Every other row is alternated by placing the tile seam halfway in between the adjacent rows of tiles.

Brickwork

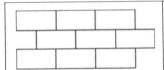

(AKA "Subway" style) – same as "Running Bond", except it applies to longer, rectangular sized tiles. "Staggered Brickwork" is a variation with only partial overlap.

Lacework

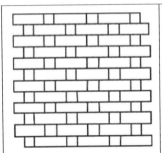

Same as "Brickwork", except that the brick-shaped tiles are alternated with square tiles half the size.

Pinwheel

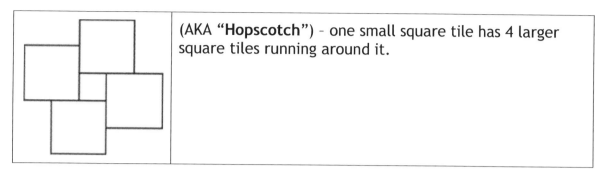

(AKA **"Hopscotch"**) – one small square tile has 4 larger square tiles running around it.

Windmill

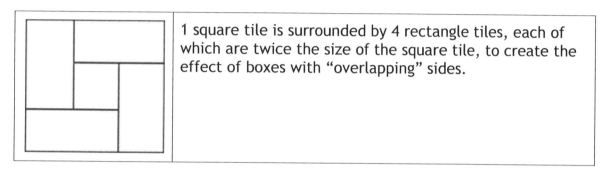

1 square tile is surrounded by 4 rectangle tiles, each of which are twice the size of the square tile, to create the effect of boxes with "overlapping" sides.

Soldiered

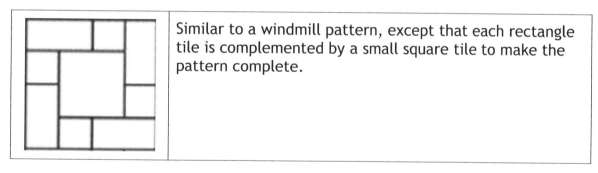

Similar to a windmill pattern, except that each rectangle tile is complemented by a small square tile to make the pattern complete.

Circular Rectangular

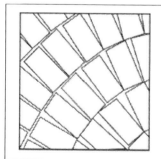

Brick-sized tiles arranged lengthwise around a circle shape.

Herringbone

 (AKA "Chevron") – long narrow tiles are placed in a "V" shape, alternating up and down.

Basketweave

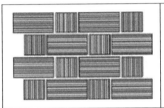 Creates the illusion of a woven basket by alternating square tiles textured vertically and rectangular tiles textured horizontally.

Brickweave

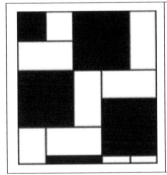 Hybrid between the "Brickwork" and "Basketweave" patterns. Uses brick-shaped tiles in a Basketweave pattern.

Hexagon

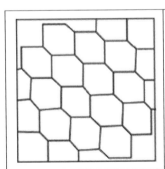 6-sided tiles are laid out with each edge touching the next. Colored tile may be used to create various patterns.

Corridor

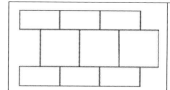 | A row of squares, alternated by a row of rectangle tiles that are half the size of the squares.

Cobblestone

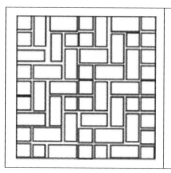 | Each "square" is composed of many rectangular and square tiles.

Interlocked

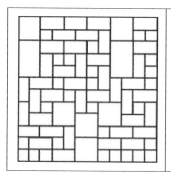 | A mixture of various sized tiles arranged in a random-looking pattern.

Mosaic

 | (AKA "Kaleidoscope") – decorative tiles of various shapes inserted to create an intricately detailed pattern.

Pentagon Diamonds

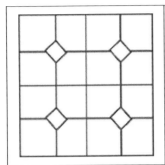

Straight grid pattern with a small square inserted in the center of the seams, and set at a diagonal angle.

3-D Diamonds

"3-D Diamond" pattern is a horizontally-oriented diamond shaped tiles, each with a trapezoid shaped tile under both sides to create a 3-D effect.

Versailles

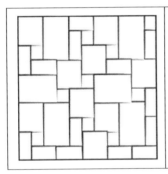

4 various sizes of tiles form a sophisticated asymmetrical pattern.

Stepping Stone

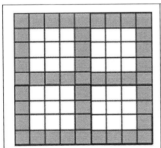

Small square tiles in a neutral color with periodic rows and columns of a bright, contrasting tile create the illusion of large, separate squares.

Border Patterns

| 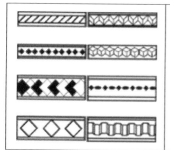 | Long tiles on the top and bottom of a running pattern, with an intricate pattern running inside the length. |

Accent

|  | Any small pattern used as an accent to a larger pattern. |

Insert

| 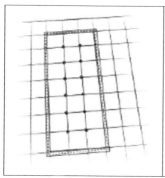 | A small pattern inserted inside of a larger pattern. For example, a grid pattern floor with a diagonal pattern inserted in the center area. |

Liner Border

| 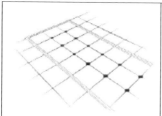 | Long, thin tiles laid end-to-end to create a running edge, often separating two tile patterns (for example, to set off the "insert" pattern; refer to above). |

Zig-Zag Border

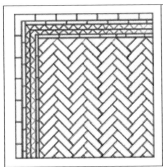 Right triangles alternated around the edge of another pattern to create a border. "Diamond Border" is another variation.

Installation

Proper installation of tile is the key to durability and assurance that it will last for many years. Enthusiastic DIY'ers may not be aware of professional installation techniques and can make rookie mistakes. These errors may not always be visible, but as the tile is used, the robustness will be tested and lack of resiliency becomes apparent. Listed below are some of the tile problems that buyers encounter.

Uneven tiles probably mean that the installer did not use the same size spacers consistently between the seams. Tiles that wiggle might mean they were not adhered using thinset mortar. Wobbly tiles could mean that the grout was not cured by waiting at least a day before using it.

Gaps between the tile floor and the wall show that the installer did not measure properly or neglected to use trimwork. An uneven drop-off between flooring types may indicate missing transition strips.

Jagged corners, too-short tile, and big gaps are indications that the tile installers did not use the proper tools. Tiles must be cut with a diamond-blade tile saw table, keeping it wet while cutting. Nippers are tools used to snip the corners, and a file is used to smooth the edges.

Cracked tiles may indicate (1) lack of proper underlayment, (2) too thin of a tile for heavy usage; or (3) a shifting slab foundation (common in California houses). As a Realtor® it's critical to spot potential problems for your buyers, and advise them of the importance of a professional home inspection.

Underlayment

Buckling, cracked, or missing tile may indicate that the tile was not installed on top of substantial underlayment, a signal of poor quality construction. Buyers should ask their home inspector to pay special attention to tile floors in this condition.

Tiles can be installed over any hard, level surface, including old vinyl or linoleum flooring, hardwood, or even the concrete foundation. However, the durability of the tile depends largely on surface prepping and underlayment.

The purpose of underlayment is to protect the floor against moisture damage, to create a smooth surface that levels out the foundation, and to absorb weight from heavy traffic. Popular underlayment includes:

- "Rubber" tile membrane (with a "waffle" grid) for floors & counters
- Kraft paper (grade "B") laminated with asphalt and aqua bar
- Backerboard (cementitious type) along with a felt moisture barrier (for shower stalls)
- Greenboard sheetrock (for walls, counters, & floors, but not water proof for shower/tub enclosures)
- Natural cork (floors) – with a waterproof membrane
- Vinyl sheet (floors)
- Plywood, chip board, or particle board – but may not be suitable for floors

Quality prep materials prevent the tile from contracting and expanding, reduce noise by absorbing sound, and inhibit mold and mildew. Look for underlayment created from natural or recycled materials.

Grout

Grout is the gritty filler mixture applied between tile seams. It dries to a hard surface (similar to concrete or stucco) and keeps the tiles in place. Grout can be either unsanded or sanded (to prevent cracking in wide seams). Silicone caulking may also be used as a grout in bathrooms near the edge of the tile.

Grout is porous (absorbs water) so it must be sealed to repel water. Sealer should be re-applied periodically to prevent mildew and erosion. Unsealed grout causes many problems in the home, such as mold in humid areas (bathroom shower walls), stains in areas with spills (kitchen counters), and deterioration in heavy-use areas (flooring).

Grout is available in a wide variety of colors, such as dark colors (to hide dirt) or colors that contrast to the tiles and creates an eye-catching pattern. Grout may also be painted with a special grout paint, so watch out for grout that looks new and clean, but it is actually old, dirty, or moldy grout that was painted over.

Alternately, tiles may be butted up next to each other without grout. This style is primarily for decorative applications, such as fireplace surrounds. Also, metal rods may be installed in the seams, rather than grout. You may see metal seams in heavy-duty commercial applications, such as airports.

Radiant Heat

Warm tiles under morning toes is a bathroom trend growing in popularity. Tile is cold and therefore not seen often in chilly climates. However, with radiant tubes installed underneath the tile to heat it, tile is gaining acceptance in the Mid-West and other cold winter climates. An under-tile heat mat is another way to install heated tiles, and should be used in conjunction with a heat-resistant underlayment.

Conclusion

With your new-found knowledge about tile, you can feel confident advertising your new luxury listing featuring a marble entryway, a travertine tile fireplace, subway tile in the shower, and recycled glass backsplash in the kitchen. And you can spot tile patterns such as pinwheel, windmill, and basketweave.

Now that you understand tile installation, you can explain to your buyers that the cracked tile could be due to incorrect installation, and may not necessarily indicate a cracked foundation. Also you can alert them to have the sparkling, glistening "white" grout in the bathroom inspected for mildew, as it appears to have been painted recently. Of course any potential issues would be verified by a home inspector, but the buyers are relying on your experience and knowledge to point out "red flags" before purchase. And that's why YOU are the best Realtor® in the neighborhood!

14. HVAC / Mechanical

View sample illustrations on our pinterest board:

http://www.pinterest.com/realtyproadvisr/hvac-mechanical

While we typically would not check "under the hood" of a house, we do verify that the visual components are available and appear to be in good condition. Here is a primer for real estate professionals who want to know what's going on behind the walls when they need to advise their buyer or seller clients.

When taking a listing, do you know what to mark in the heat/cooling fields? Learning the HVAC components will help you understand and describe your listing. When working for your buyer clients, product knowledge equips you to recognize defects and negotiate repairs shown on a home inspection.

HVAC stands for "Heating, Ventilation, and Air Conditioning" which refers to the air coming into, going out of, and circulating through a house. System components include a furnace (heater), air ducts, vents, filters, and optionally a cooling system. The HVAC system is designed for health and comfort. This acronym is pronounced "H - vac" or "H-V-A-C". Let's take a look at components that are the basic mechanical systems in a residential house.

Heating & Furnaces

Furnaces are mandatory — they must be installed and operable, per government guidelines. Legally, residential house MUST have a permanent heat source. A plug-in room heater will not suffice.

A furnace is the technical name for a heater. Heating fuel includes gas, oil, propane, coal, and electricity. Heat sources may consist of:

- Electric
- Natural Gas
- Propane
- Coal
- Pellets
- Wood
- Solar
- Air
- Hot water
- Steam

Fuel sourced furnaces (gas and oil) require a pilot light to stay lit, and must exhaust the gases to the exterior of the building. An electric furnace uses heating elements to warm the air. Wood and coal furnaces burn the fuel in a sealed firebox. Older homes may have an oil tank in the basement or buried underground, which will eventually leak or deteriorate and be hazardous environmentally.

Forced Air Unit (FAU)

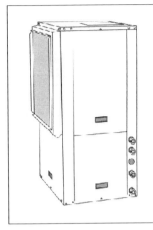 The most common type of central heating, FAU consists of a furnace that generates heat, which is then blown throughout the house via ducts and vents. The furnace may be located in the attic, basement / crawl space, or closet. The closet-type furnace may be located either inside or outside the house. If located outside, it pulls in exterior air and may be less of a carbon monoxide threat for residents. **FAG (forced air gas) and FAE (forced air electric) are common abbreviations on home inspections.**

Wall Heater

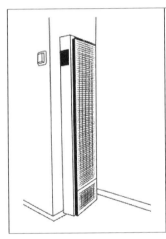 Permanently installed **wall heaters** are usually gas-fueled, but may also run on electric power. Often seen in homes built between 1950 and 1970 because then builders switched to central HVAC systems. Wall heaters are viewed as inferior to central HVAC systems, since the heat is disbursed from only 1 location. The thermostat is either on the wall next to the heater, or within the bottom of the heater itself.

Fireplace / Wood Burning Stove

 Although a fireplace or wood stove may radiate a lot of heat, it will not be the primary source of heat for a residential home. Fireplaces that burn wood often disburse ashes and dust throughout the house, which can be detrimental to asthma sufferers. Stoves may also burn fuel-efficient pellets rather than wood.

Radiant Heating

Radiant heating is a system of water tubes (hydronic) or electrically heated pipes underneath the floor. Although it heats a room slowly, the room stays warm for quite a while because the heat rises to the ceiling. These systems are rare but may be found in condos that are built with electricity as the only power source. Also seen in home renovations for specific rooms, such as under tile floor in a bathroom.

Floor Furnace

In older houses, the furnace may be located under the house, often in an old-fashioned fuel boiler, and send the heat up through the floor with a vent located in the middle of the house. The large metal vent can get quite hot, which may be dangerous for residents walking on bare feet!

Propane Tank

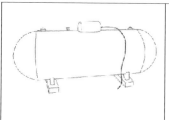

In rural areas without gas utility pipes to the property, residents will usually have an outdoor propane tank that feeds fuel into the house. It must be filled by a professional propane company and maintained by the homeowners. The tank will eventually rust due to exposure to outdoor elements.

Radiator

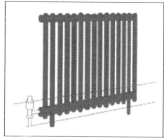

An old-time radiator is a metal heater that contains water or radiator fluid. When turned on, it heats up the liquid and disburses heat. Radiators heat a specific space, usually only 1 room, and can take quite a while to warm a room. They are usually seen in houses that were built over a century ago.

Baseboard Heaters

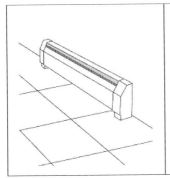

Built into the baseboard, these small, long heaters are usually powered by electricity. They are often added into rooms in older homes that were built without central heat or as supplemental heat sources for add-on rooms.

Boiler

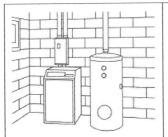

Boilers are rare, but may be seen in older houses, especially on the East Coast.

Air Conditioning & Cooling

Residential houses are not required to have air conditioning or cooling capabilities, even in the desert with 120° hot summers. Just like with furnaces, optional cooling devices range from inexpensive portable "swamp coolers" to complex whole-house multi-level auto-adjusting air conditioning systems. Air conditioning systems are ranked by SEER (Seasonal Energy Efficiency Rating). EER (Energy Efficiency Rating) and Energy Star both measure energy efficiency. "A/C" is a common abbreviation for Air Conditioner.

Central Forced Air

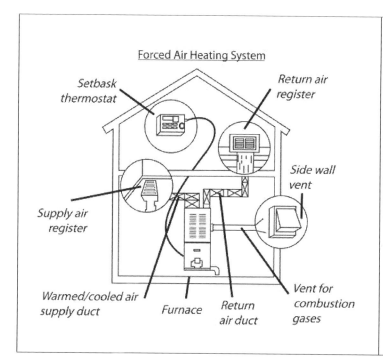

Forced air systems pull in air, cool it, and then distribute throughout the house via ducts and vents. Central or whole-house air conditioning systems are common in areas that are either hot, or warm and humid. Residential central air conditioners are usually split systems — the condenser and compressor are outside the building, while the evaporator operates in the house.

Evaporative Coolers

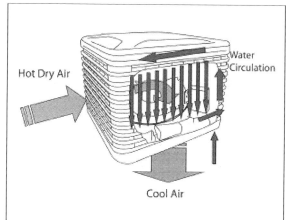

Evaporative "swamp" coolers – installed in a window or a wall – can be portable. They operate quite efficient as they draw in outdoor air and cool it over water-filled pads. These units "leak" onto the ground as they dispense used water and may not be visually appealing. They only cool one room at a time, so multiple coolers will be needed throughout the house. They are viewed as inferior to central forced air systems.

Attic Fan

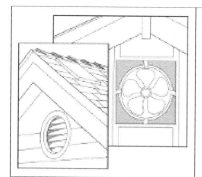

An attic fan works very efficiently by sucking in the hot air at the ceiling or attic level, and expelling it from the house. It then re-circulates the cooler air into the home.

Chiller

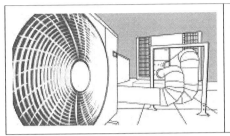

A chiller operates by distributing cold water to air cooling coils via pipes throughout the house. It also includes a hot water boiler for the heating system, with separate pipes for hot and cold water. Although expensive, chillers are highly energy efficient.

Fans and Ventilation

Ceiling fans, as part of a light fixture, can be installed in most any house. Other fans may include bathroom exhaust fans, range exhaust fans, and wall louvers for summer time cooling. In addition to cooling, fans help to circulate clean air.

Other cooling systems include:

Gas air conditioner

Electric air conditioner also known as a swap cooler

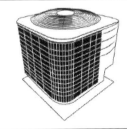

Heat Pump (water source or electric) – sits outside the house

Ventilation & Air Distribution System

Besides the heating and cooling components, the ventilation system is comprised of vents, registers, filters, ducts, and thermostats.

Vents & Registers

In a central air ventilation system, common in most California homes, fans pull in the air through a register, heat the air, and then blow it into the house through small vents. When inspecting the house, often you will observe a large intake vent in the ceiling which leads to the furnace in the attic. Sometimes the intake is a series of small registers in the floor or on the wall. Observe the vents — do they have filters? Are the filters dirty? Are the filters inhibiting air flow?

Ducts

The air is distributed through ducts, usually in an attic or crawl space under a house. The air quality of the home is determined by the intake air, and also by the cleanliness of the ducts, and how well they are connected to each other. A duct system that harbors mold or bacteria could have a toxic effect on its residents. Likewise, ductwork that is deteriorated, broken, or inhabited by rodents can pull unwanted elements into the house.

Thermostats

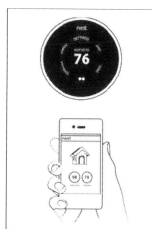

The furnace and cooling system is controlled by a thermostat. Tech savvy thermostats regulate heat automatically or remotely from a smart phone. Newer programmable thermostats can save substantial energy costs.

Air Quality

Besides regulating heat, cold air, and air flow, a mechanical system can help control humidity. Accessories can be added to HVAC systems to improve the air quality and enhance circulation. Some indoor air quality options include:

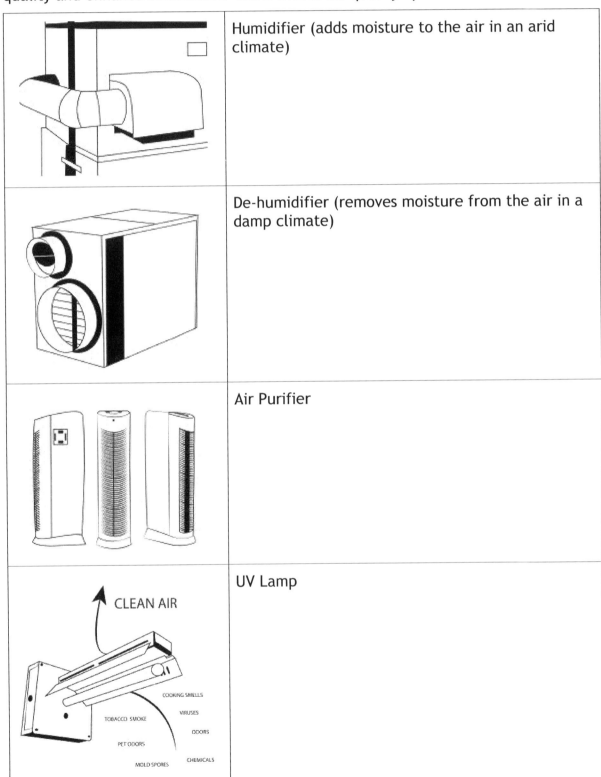

	Humidifier (adds moisture to the air in an arid climate)
	De-humidifier (removes moisture from the air in a damp climate)
	Air Purifier
	UV Lamp

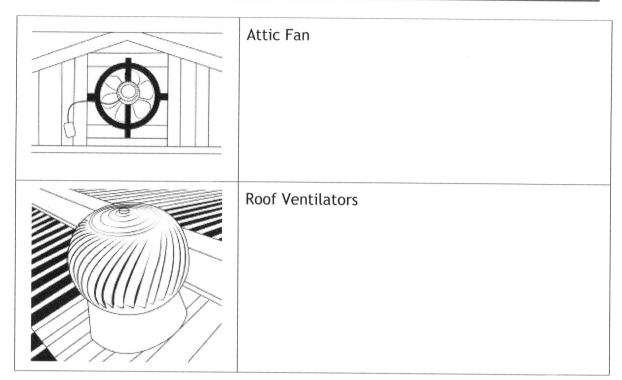

	Attic Fan
	Roof Ventilators

Optimal air ventilation can eliminate allergens to reduce allergy attacks, and help asthma sufferers better control incidents. A HEPA air filter can be easily added to a central HVAC system.

System Types

HVAC systems may be installed as packaged systems, zoned systems, split systems, duct-free split systems, and hybrid heat systems. A zoned system means that specific areas of the house have individual controls which heat/cool only certain rooms, saving money and energy.

The split system is most popular in residential houses. It has an indoor furnace and an air conditioner that sits outside the building, with air ducts installed throughout the home. Less popular is the **packaged system that accommodates smaller houses.** A **h**ybrid system is a gas furnace heater with the addition of an electric heating or A/C system. Compare that to a duct-free system, which is a heat pump or A/C with a fan coil.

In hot humid areas, single stage cooling is popular, as is single stage heating in cold winter climates. However, single stage is not the most efficient, because it means that the HVAC system is running full blast around the clock. They can save energy costs by upgrading to a multi-stage system and by installing Energy Star Certified appliances.

GREEN Conversion

Converting a home to GREEN energy can save both money and environmental pollutants. Because they can reduce energy bills, GREEN homes offer advantages to buyers, and therefore may be valued higher by sellers and appraisers.

Geothermal

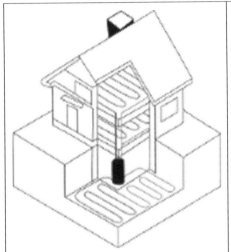

Geothermal energy harnesses the earth's natural heat below the surface. Heat pumps route tubing under the ground to warm the liquid in the pipes and capture the natural heat, which is usually a constant temperature year-round. During warm summer months, the system cools the home by reversing the heat exchange.

Solar

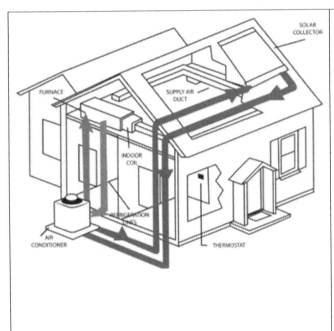

Two types of solar systems, passive and active, are being adapted for home energy power. Both collect energy from the sun, which is a renewal energy source that never runs out. "Passive solar" means installing pipes in walls and floors to gather and store energy. Windows also can be used to capture the sun's rays. "Active solar" means installing panels or solar cells on the roof. The power collected with a photovoltaic system is then stored and distributed through the home's mechanical system as heat. A new technology uses water or air to absorb solar energy, which is more efficient and less expensive. Watch for scientific developments.

Biodiesel

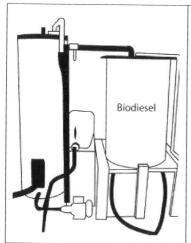

Biodiesel is a fuel blend of organic biofuel mixed combined with heating oil. Biofuels are sustainable because they are produced from corn, soy beans, wheat, and sugar cane crops. The main benefit is that the environment receives less pollutants.

Hydronic Heating

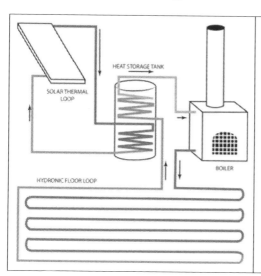

Hydronic (water) heaters transfer liquid heat through convection, conduction, or radiation. The liquid heats radiators, floors, or baseboards similar to the old-fashioned radiators, but is heated with solar or geothermal energy.

Absorption

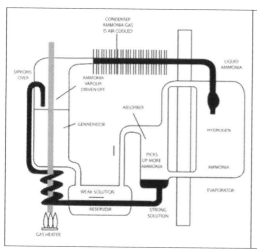

An absorption heating and cooling system uses solar, geothermal, or gas power and operates similar to a regular heat pump. However, it uses ammonia instead of a refrigerant as the heating/cooling liquid in the pipes.

Ice-Powered Air Conditioner

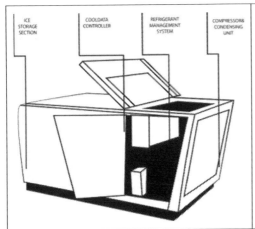

Ice Energy company is leading a GREEN revolution! The machine makes ice at night, which cools the air conditioning system during the day.

Green Coal

Coal, often viewed as a toxic fuel, can actually be environmentally friendly. With a gasification process, the carbon in the coal is used to strip oxygen from water and create clean-burning hydrogen gas, which is used for fuel. The emissions and pollutants are disposed using eco-conscious techniques.

Wind Power

Wind turbines are being developed smaller and more efficiently, and can actually generate heat for a water heater. Using magnets and magnetic resistance with copper plates, this sustainable energy source can be a permanent heat source for a house.

Biomass

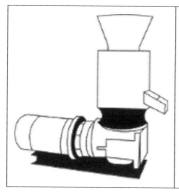
Energy that is produced from living organisms, trees for example, is known as biomass. This natural and renewable energy source converts stored energy from the sun into heat energy. Woodchip systems, for example, emit less pollutants than wood stoves and produce fewer carbon dioxide than gas or oil.

Conclusion

Now you know the HVAC lingo for houses. Your experience is showing! The next time you take a listing, show a house to a buyer, or read a home inspection report, you'll be prepared with the right terms at the tip of your tongue.

15. Ceilings

View sample illustrations on our pinterest board:

http://www.pinterest.com/realtyproadvisr/ceilings

Look up! What do you see on the ceiling? Acoustic (popcorn ceilings) or flat drywall are most common. But let's learn about other types of ceilings you may see while listing a property for sale — or showing homes to prospective buyers.

A ceiling is the interior surface of a roof, with insulation sandwiched in between the two. Its purpose is to protect the residents from the elements (rain, sun, wind, and snow) while adding an architectural element to the interior.

Ceiling heights vary, but a typical height is 8 feet. Dropped ceilings, especially in kitchens, may have a height less than 8 feet. Houses built before standardized building codes and tract homes, add-on rooms, and attics often have lower ceilings.

Upscale homes usually feature raised ceilings or soaring ceiling heights of 12 feet or higher. Taller ceilings are desirable because they convey a spacious, open feeling. However, they are more difficult to manage (clean, paint, and change light bulbs) and cost more energy for heating/cooling.

Acoustic "Popcorn" Ceiling

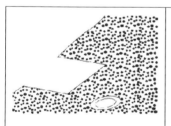

What's the first thing new buyers do when they move into a house built in the 1960's or 70's? Scrape off that outdated popcorn ceiling! A staple of early tract houses, these ceilings were the victims of mass spray-on texturing. But be careful with removal, because popcorn ceilings may contain asbestos. Popular then, but now officially out of style, they are sometimes referred to as "orange peel" ceilings.

Arched Ceiling

Curves upwards steeply to create a coved arch look. The rising ceiling conveys a formal elegance and luxury. An arched ceiling may have multiple arches repeating throughout a hallway. They are often placed in conjunction with arched doorways and windows to echo the steep arched style.

Attic Ceiling

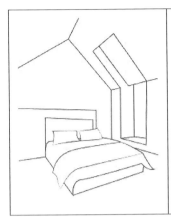

Lower along the roofline, an attic ceiling may not meet the building code requirements for a room that can be occupied as a bedroom. Common in areas such as the East Coast, Mid-West, and South, attic ceilings are usually found in tall houses with semi-usable attics. Many rooms are converted from attic space to semi-living areas, which means tall people may bump their heads because the side ceilings are so low.

Barrel Vault Ceiling

The ceiling curves upward, gently rounding into a semicircle or a partial dome shape. Commonly seen in formal rooms of mansions or great rooms, the ceiling may be highlighted with a curved wooden beam. It's called a barrel vault because the shape resembles the inside of a partial barrel. A variation of the vaulted ceiling, it is also known as a wagon vault or tunnel vault.

Box Beam Ceiling

Wooden cross beams in a rectangular pattern are visible on the ceiling. The beams resemble a decorative tic-tac-toe grid. They can be painted, but are most often stained to highlight the wood's natural grain. The recessed ceiling space in between the beams may be crafted of wood, drywall, tiles, or lighting. Box beam ceilings are most effective in a room with tall ceiling height. They are a type of coffered ceiling.

Cathedral Ceiling

Named after churches, or cathedrals, these ceilings are symmetrical (the same on both sides) and slope at a steep pitch. Both sides meet at a top ridge. Cathedral ceilings are treasured for their dramatic effect. The ceiling emulates the roof's pitch, structure, and style. The beams are usually visible; the ceiling often IS the roof. In other words, there is no additional layer of insulation between the roof and the ceiling. Often confused with a vaulted ceiling.

Coffered Ceiling

Wooden beam in a unique design. Similar to a box beam ceiling, except the beams are can be arranged in any type of geometric pattern. The recessed panels between beams may be decorative. A formal, elegant look for an upscale home, the coffers (wooden beams) may be crafted from other wood-looking materials. Molding trim, medallions, and ornaments may be applied to heighten the theatrical aspect.

Combination Ceiling

A ceiling constructed with two or more different styles. For example, a vaulted ceiling may have one side comprised of wooden panels, and the other side drywall.

Cove Ceiling

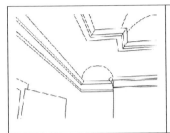

The sides of the ceiling (where it meets the wall) are finished with a curved plaster molding. The molding is much wider than a simple wooden strip of trim. A coved ceiling adds character and charm. The coving and the ceiling are often painted contrasting colors to create a feeling of depth.

Cross-Vaulted Ceiling

A type of vaulted ceiling wherein the cross-beams intersect each other at an angle. It produces a stunning 3-dimensional effect. The arches may either be round or pointed. Also known as groin vaults.

Domed Ceiling

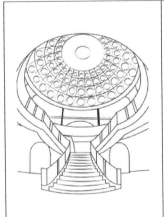

A round, circle-shaped ceiling that rises in the middle, like an upside-down bowl. It may simulate an antique church or other historic building. To create a heavenly feeling, the dome may have (or appear to have) a glass skylight (called an "oculus") or stained glass. This ceiling style is an astounding breath-taking feature that captures attention.

Flat Ceiling

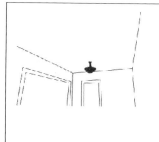

A level ceiling with no pitch. This is the typical type of ceiling for most homes, especially tract houses. The ceiling is often finished with drywall, and covered with paint or texture. Because of the distance between the roof and the ceiling, there is plenty of attic space to insulate the home. Flat ceilings may also be made of plaster (common in older houses) or other materials.

Floating / Drop-Down Ceiling

A single piece of ceiling hangs down below the rest of the flat ceiling. The "floating" piece is hung from the flat ceiling with wires. The floating piece may contain lighting, both direct lighting and uplighting, for a 2-part effect. This modern design, borrowed from commercial buildings, is also known as a drop-down ceiling. Note, however, that it is not the same as a suspended/dropped grid ceiling.

Drywall Ceiling

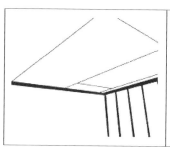

The most common type of ceiling in a house. It is comprised of drywall/sheetrock panels that are nailed onto the ceiling trusses and beams. The seams are taped and sanded before finishing with paint. The flat, white ceilings are then painted or textured. Other finishes, such as wallpaper or stencils, may be applied.

Open / Exposed Beam Ceiling

As the name implies, the wooden roof trusses and beams are visible (exposed) and become part of the ceiling. The soaring ceiling with natural lumber imparts a rustic style to cabins and vacation retreat homes. However, since the attic is missing, there is no roof insulation. Also, it takes more to heat a larger space, so energy bills may be higher. Compare to a cathedral ceiling or a vaulted ceiling.

Glass Tile Ceiling

Glass tiles, often colored or bearing a leaded glass pattern, are hung in between box beams. The are lit from above to they bring a sense of light and warmth into a room. Either contemporary or antique styled, glass tiled ceilings are often incorporated into other ceiling types. Although rare in residential homes, they are becoming more popular as an eclectic style.

Metal Tiles / Tin Ceiling

Square metal tiles are glued or nailed to the ceiling to create a stunning old-fashioned effect. The traditional tin tiles are crafted from tin-plated steel. They are primed and painted on both sides to avert metal corrosion. Plastic faux-metal tiles, and other types of metals, can be used to create the "tin" look.

Painted Mosaic

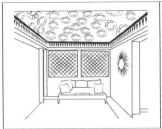

A mosaic design-inspired artwork painted across the breadth of the ceiling. It could be a single picture, a repeating design, or a custom art collection. A hand-painted ceiling is a fresh alternative to wallpaper.

Retractable Sunroof

A bedroom sunroof sheds light during the day and closes at night; but it retracts for viewing the moon at stars at night. A star-gazing sunroof allows the residents to relax and view the starry night sky from their warm cozy bed. A retractable sunroof in a bedroom is truly a unique home feature.

Suspended Ceiling

A metal grid is hung below the ceiling, with panels setting in between each grid. This is a non-structural (secondary) ceiling. Popular in commercial and industrial buildings because it conceals pipes and wires, it could spell trouble when seen in a residential home. A suspended ceiling may have been used to hide roof leaks or other ceiling problems. In some cases, it hides the beautiful original ceiling. One bonus is that a suspended may add a sound barrier. Also known as a dropped ceiling, some panels may be clear and have lights above them. NOT the same as a drop-down / floating ceiling (above).

Textured / Plaster Ceiling

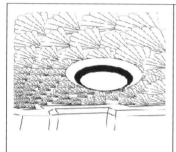

A flat drywall or plaster ceiling may be enriched by applying texture. Texture is a filling applied in a pattern that adds dimension or a raised surface. The filling is applied with a trowel, roller, or hand-dabbed to achieve an effect such as an arch, shell, or dabble. The textured ceiling may be hiding previous water leaks, or may have been added simply for the charm and character it imparts.

Textured Panels

Manufactured homes, such as mobile homes or pre-fabricated kit houses, often have long, wide textured panels that span the length of each room. Each panel is uniform and consist due to manufacturing standards. With manufactured homes, they are inserted at the factory. They are often made from lightweight materials and may not provide much insulation. Usually, they are not painted. Another type of textured panel is a square-looking tile.

Tray Ceiling

The center area of a ceiling that is recessed. Variations may include recessed lights and molding. By adding another dimension, it creates architectural character. Tray ceilings are usually found in common living areas such as formal dining rooms. An inverted tray ceiling is just the opposite: The center area hangs lower than the sides. This is an effective way to highlight something on the ceiling, such as a pot rack over the kitchen island. A tray ceiling is similar to a cove ceiling.

Double Tray Ceiling

A variation of the tray ceiling, it is 2 steps of "trays" that creates 3 levels of ceiling height. It often pinpoints a beautiful light fixture or other artwork. A double tray ceiling can add texture with multiple layers of molding, and can be enhanced with colors and trim. Think of a framed picture with 2 layers of matting.

Vaulted Ceiling

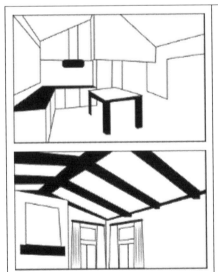

High pitched ceilings that peak at the top. They are usually framed using scissor trusses. The beams and trusses may be covered with drywall and a layer of insulation between the roof and the ceiling. The sides aren't always symmetrical. Vaulted ceilings make any room feel more spacious. They are very conducive large skylight installation. However, without adequate ventilation, vaulted ceilings can waste substantial energy due to heat rising to the ceiling. Also known as a raised ceiling and sometimes confused with a cathedral ceiling.

Virtual Window Ceiling

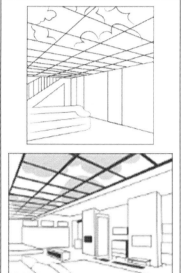

It's a screened panel with an outdoor picture that gives the illusion of the open sky. Sky Factory, a leading virtual window company, offers jaw-dropping products such as their proprietary SkyCeilings. Commonly seen in rectangular shapes, the panels can also be made in circular and custom-sized panels. Panels may be backlit with LED or fluorescent lights to produce a realistic looking sky.

Wallpaper

Applied from rolls of wallpaper, a ceiling may be decorated with a variety of colorful patterns. Especially dramatic with tray ceilings and barrel ceilings when the wallpaper echos the walls. Difficult to apply and remove, wallpaper can create an upscale look when used sparingly.

Window Ceiling

Clear glass windows create both a roof and a ceiling. Often seen in sunrooms or conservatories, they bring precious daylight into a semi-outdoor room. However, at night, they are dark. These clear glass panels, specially designed to be thick enough to preserve the structural integrity of a roof, can be also used as walls to create a room surrounded by nature.

Wood Ceiling

 Made of wood, ceilings can reflect a variety of designs. Wood ceilings can be made from planks, beadboard, or tongue-in-groove carpentry. Solid wood is a heavy material so the house must be engineered to holds its weight. Natural wood can be painted or stained. If the wood is treated, it will last for many decades. Beadboard panels are sometimes seen in attics (on the low sidewall ceilings).

Conclusion

Now that you can identify ceiling types, you can walk your buyers through properties with confidence. And when taking that elusive luxury listing, you can boast about your home's stunning ceiling features. Who knows ceilings better than you, the local real estate expert!

16. Roof Architecture

View sample illustrations on our pinterest board:

http://www.pinterest.com/realtyproadvisr/roofs

More than just a cover from the rain and insulation from the cold, roofs add aesthetic value to the character of a home. They help define the home's architectural style and determine its curb appeal. A stylish roof can soften the silhouette and add charm. An upscale roof elevates the street façade for the entire neighborhood.

Roof Architectural Styles

We're going to walk through the many types of roof architecture. Although a knowledge of roof architecture is not required to take a listing, knowledge of your product sets you above your competitors. When you understand all about roofs, you can advise your sellers and educate your buyers.

Gable Roof

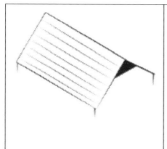	This basic roof type has 2 sloping sides which meet at the top to form a peak (ridge). It's popular because it is simple to build, offers ventilation on the ends, and the sloped sides protect the house from water and snow. The open gable has no ends, whereas the box gable has end pieces. A stepped gable means that the ends appear as stairs, as is common with New Mexico pueblo styles.

Winged Gable

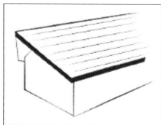	This is a variation of the gable roof. The only difference is that the top of each side (at the peak) is longer than the bottom, creating more protection over the ends of the house. Each side is paragon-shaped rather than a rectangle-shaped.

Barn Roof

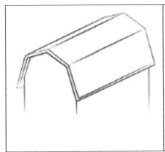

This roof is constructed using 4 pieces, 2 per side. It forms a peak at the top, but then wraps down the sides. This allows more headroom in the attic area. Often called a "barn roof" because it is typically seen on barns because they do not require much attic ventilation. Also known as a gambrel roof (not to be confused with a gable roof).

Hip Roof

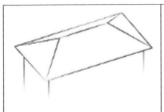

This common roof type has 4 sides that begin at the peak. The 2 longest sides meet at the top to form a peak. The style looks more sophisticated than a gable roof, but it does not allow ventilation on the ends. The pyramid hip roof means that all 4 sides are the same size and shape.

Dutch Hip Roof

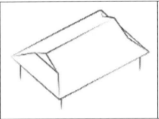

This type is a variation of the hip roof. It has the same 4 sides, except that the end pieces each have a gable (small window). In addition to creating character, the gables provide ventilation.

Round Hip Roof

This circle-shaped roof is found on round buildings, such as Deltec homes. Each piece is a pie-shaped wedge, which forms a round octagonal pattern. The corners meet and peak in the middle to allow water drainage down all sides. This roof type is known for high resistance to hurricane winds. Also called a geometric hip roof, 360° hip roof, and continuous hip roof.

Hip & Valley Roof

This style combines several hip roofs at various levels. It creates charm and character but has more potential for roof leaks, due to the many adjoining peaks, both upward and downward.

Mansard Roof

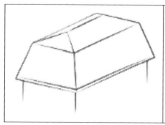

This French design is similar to a hip roof, in that it has 4 sides. The difference is that each side has 2 pieces. This creates less attic headroom as it wraps down each of the 4 sides, similar to a barn roof.

Flat Roof

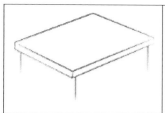

This single-piece roof is completely flat. It is the cheapest to build but offers minimal shielding from the elements. Flat roofs are not recommended because they aren't designed for drainage, and can cause roof water leaks.

Shed Roof

Similar to a flat roof, it is only one piece. However, it's installed on a sloped angle so the rain and snow drip off naturally. A great option for "green" building, the opposite side of the house can accommodate large windows for natural sunlight. Alternatively, 2 shed roofs can be installed on opposite sides of the house at different levels, allowing for large windows on the wall between both roofs. Also known as a skillion roof, lean-to roof, or mono-pitched roof.

A-Frame Roof

This roof has 2 long sides which meet to form a peak at the top, similar to the gable roof. However, the sides have a steeper slope and are much longer, often reaching down towards the bottom of the house in an upside-down V shape. This distinctive style is often seen on mountain cabins because it prevents snow build-up.

Saltbox Roof

 Popular on the East Coast, it has 2 pieces similar to the gable roof, except that one side extends down much longer than the other side. In the New England region, an addition was added onto one side of the house, and then the roof would be extended to cover the addition. It soon became an architectural wonder.

Dormer Roof

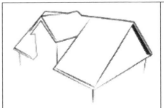 This means it has a dormer window in the side of the roof. Popular in East Coast and Mid-West construction, where most houses have attics.

Pagoda Roof

 Adapted from the Chinese and other Asian cultures, this style curves upwards at the corners. Legends say it is for good luck because it repels evil spirits, but the design is actually very functional for column-constructed homes. While large overhangs deflect rain and sunlight, it allows the entry of fresh air and removal of smoke exhaust through the central roof column. Also known as an upturned roof, it showcases distinctive artistic designs.

Butterfly Roof

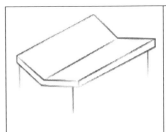 This style, like the gable roof, also has 2 sides. However, the sides meet in the middle going downwards, which is the reverse style of a gable roof. The pro is that large windows can be installed on both sides of the house, capturing natural light. The con is that water drains to the middle of the roof and is a potential source of roof leaks.

Curved Roof

This upside-down U-shaped roof is often used for metal sheds and barns, but is also seen on specialty construction homes. This single-piece construction prevents roof leaks because there are no seams at the peak. Variations include a partial U-shape that slopes more gently.

Curved Panel Roof

This is a series of curved roofs (see above) that span the distance of the building. Most often seen on metal commercial buildings.

Folded Plate Roof

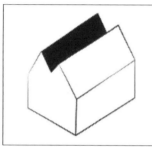

This accordion-shaped style is generally seen on commercial buildings rather than residential. Also known as an M-shaped roof.

Double Tier Roof

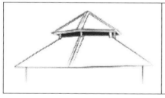

This refined styled has two eves, with a smaller roof on top of a larger roof. The purpose is to allow for attic ventilation, especially on a round roof. It also evokes aesthetic charm.

Pent Roof

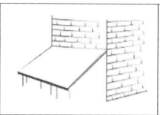

Refers to a short overhang inserted into a wall. It is not a true "roof" but helps to provide shade and water runoff. It also adds an architectural element of character on a multi-story house.

Hybrid Roof

	Many top tier homes boast roofs that combine several different styles. This classy look radiates charm and curb appeal, especially when designed by a renowned architect.

Contemporary Styles

	Modern, eclectic homes may have unique contemporary roofs. Examples include parasol roof, warped roof, or free-form roof.

Roof Materials

Residential roofs in California are most often constructed from composition asphalt shingles ("comp"). Red clay or concrete tiles are popular on Spanish style homes. Fiber cement, a heavy-duty roof, is known to be fire proof. Less effective roofs include wood shingles / shakes (flame-retardant), tar / rolled (hot mopped onto flat roof), rock / gravel (usually on top of tar) and metal (aluminum or steel).

As you are learning about roofs, you will also begin learning the various components, such as trusses / rafters, ventilation, flashing, insulation, gutters, drain spouts, fascia (under eaves), sheathing, and attic access.

Summary

When we take a listing and enter it into the MLS, we need to identify the type of roof on the house. Is it composition shingle, clay tile, or metal? Hopefully you remembered to LOOK UP when you were at the property meeting with the sellers! If not, review the photos you took from the street view. You may surprise yourself by recognizing the roof's architectural style.

17. GREEN Eco-Conscious

View sample illustrations on our pinterest board:

http://www.pinterest.com/realtyproadvisor/green-home-features

The decade's hottest topic is GREEN living. We've learned to recycle, right? Everyone's talking about renewable energy. Clients want to know about tax rebates for appliances. GREEN homes are definitely an increasing trend.

Years ago, a home with no utility bills was generally rural property "off the grid". At that time, we never could have imagined an off-the-grid home in a regular suburban tract neighborhood. But then again, we never would have dreamed how high utility bills could soar, either!

Lower utility bills is just one advantage of going green. Other green home benefits may include: superior air quality, tax benefits or credits, relief from allergies or asthma, and a year-round comfortable climate. A positive contribution to the environment is always a feel-good feature too. And yes, homes with substantial GREEN features can be more valuable when selling!

As REALTORS® we are always on the cutting edge of new technology and housing upgrades. What better way to provide value than to understand sustainable features.

GREEN Terms

Let's first review the many GREEN terms being circulated.

Green

Does green mean it's green in color? Not really. "Green" or GREEN homes refer to housing that uses less water, energy, and materials, minimizes the environmental impact, and improves human health. These buildings reduce the fossil fuel burning, so they generate less air pollution. Going "green" may refer to any the terms below.

Eco-Conscious / Eco-Friendly / Nature Friendly

Being aware of, and reducing the impact on, ecological resources. Concern about environmental responsibility and planning ahead to reduce harm on the environment and natural ecosystems. This includes wildlife, landscape, and natural habitats.

Energy-Saving / Energy Efficient

Products that reduce consumption from existing power sources. It may include products that are modified to save energy, as well as newly manufactured products designed specifically for energy savings. Refer to the section, "Rating Types".

Sustainable

Sustainable properties are inclusive, self-sufficient homes and land that account for all of their own needs without drawing resources from others. Sustainable development meets this generation's current needs without compromising the needs of future generations. The sustainable movement has picked up speed amongst global leaders with the common goal of global self-sufficiency, beginning in every community worldwide.

Architectural Styles

New eco-friendly homes are being built that embrace comfort and convenience while incorporating recycled or green products at an affordable cost. Homes may also incorporate solar greenhouses for gardening, and cellars (food pantries naturally cooled by the earth). Families who want to "live lightly" and conserve resources while still being cozy can select from several architectural design plans below.

EarthShip

A self-sustainable hip home, EarthShip begins with old tires stacked like bricks, then transformed into earth walls. The design boasts a wall of windows to welcome daylight and create an indoor garden. Passive solar provides energy while saving utility bills. Ecology-saving plumbing features include roof water catchment, composting toilets, and greywater.

Geodesic Dome

 As a kid, remember using wooden sticks and round pegs to build a sphere? A geodesic dome home is the same concept: hexagons, pentagons, and triangles form a rigid dome-shaped building exterior. It's stronger than traditional construction because the stress points are distributed evenly across the structure. Home builders can even buy a dome home kit and assemble it themselves. Sort of like when you were a kid, but much more exciting!

Round House

 Circular style homes, although octagonal rather than perfectly curved, are becoming more popular in rural areas. They function much like a traditional home, but are built from a factory kit, so the construction can include green building materials. The rounded design protects against strong winds, and the enormous windows offer sunlight and passive solar energy.

Earth Sheltered / Earth Bermed

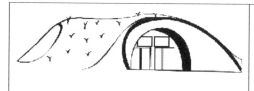 "Earth bermed" is a home above grade, with earth built up against an exterior wall. A home built underground, with 3 side walls and the roof buried, is called "earth sheltered". The dirt wall nestled against the building is a natural insulator that regulates the home's temperate to ensure a moderate interior climate year-round. Earth walls increase privacy, reduce noise, and ensure that the house won't freeze even in the winter! Bermed homes are landscaped to blend in with the surrounding environment. They may feature an atrium entrance with glass walls and living roof with plants growing on it.

Renewable Energy

Energy that is produced naturally and abundantly in nature includes wind, sunlight, and geothermal heat. Forces of nature such as waves, tides, and rain can also be harnessed for energy output. Energy typically used in a home includes electricity, hot water heater, and furnace/heaters. Renewal energy can generate enough alternative power to fuel all of these outputs.

Fuel Cell

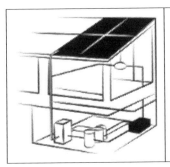

Fuel cells are a source of clean fuel that yields zero emissions by converting chemical energy from hydrogen to electrical energy. Look for substantial future developments in this area of science as technology increases the capability of fuel cells.

Geothermal Heat

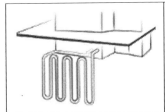

Geothermal heat is created with pipes that go deep underground to capture the earth's natural heat (or coldness) and route that into a home. Fluid is pumped through pipes to keep the heat (or coldness) flowing up to the surface.

Photovoltaic / Solar Panel

Photovoltaic cells (PV) harness the power of sunlight to generate electricity from solar panels, frequently installed on the roof. Newer types are lighter and more efficient. Homeowners may realize substantially less expensive power bills, and also benefit from tax credits.

Wind Power

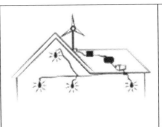

Tall turbines capture the wind and convert the kinetic energy into mechanical power. A "wind farm" full of turbines can generate enough electricity to power entire cities. Small stand-alone turbines (modern version of the classic wind mill) are used for tasks such as pumping water or grinding grain. AKA Wind energy or Wind generated power.

Rating Types

As the housing industry evolved to embrace the environmental movement, certifications and ratings have popped up. Here's a guide to help you decipher the industry ratings that may be applied to a house.

BPI Rating

Building Performance Institute (BPI) is an organization that cultivates high standards in energy efficiency for home renovations. They train and certify GREEN workers who follow protocol for high performance. BPI certified professionals contribute to improving the health, comfort, durability, safety, and energy efficiency of houses. BPI standards are even required for some State-run energy efficient and weatherization assistance programs.

BuildIt Green Certified

BuildIt Green is a nonprofit that increases awareness and adoption of green building practices. They promote healthy, energy- and resource-efficient building practices through outreach and education. BuildIt Green provides a brand, GreenPoint Rated, to help consumers choose authentic green products and offers a GREEN training program for real estate agents.

Energy Star Qualified

Appliances verified as Energy Star must be at least 15% more energy efficient and incorporate additional energy-saving features that are 20-30% more efficient than standard homes. The EPA (U.S. Environmental Protection Agency) sets the guidelines. Houses can also earn the blue Energy Star label if they meet the EPA guidelines. Features include efficient walls, windows, air ducts, heating equipment, lights, and appliances.

HERS Rated

The Home Energy Rating System (HERS) index measures a house's energy efficiency by using a formula to calculate its energy performance. The HERS system is nationally recognized and regarded as the industry standard report. A certified rater assesses the home's energy efficiency and assigns a performance score. The lower the number, the more energy efficient the home.

"When you're selling your home, a low HERS Index Score can command a higher resale price. And when you're buying a home you can anticipate the costs of energy bills and efficiency upgrades," according to RESNET, the Residential Energy Services Network. The HERS index guide is listed at www.resnet.us/hers-index.

Indoor airPLUS

This label, created by the EPA, applies to qualifying Energy Star homes that contain 60 additional construction and design features to protect home owners from mold, toxic chemicals, pests, radon, and other airborne pollutants. The Indoor airPLUS standard is the most stringent of all specifications.

LEED Certified

LEED (Leadership in Energy & Environmental Design) certification is recognized as the leading industry standard for building energy efficient homes. Buildings must incorporate green practices and building strategies to earn various ratings of certification.

WaterSense®

High quality products that save water can earn the WaterSense® label from the EPA. These plumbing materials are highly efficient and save at least 20% more water. The WaterSense® label makes it simple for home owners to select environmentally friendly products when remodeling their homes.

A Green home is built using energy-efficient resources and environmentally responsible processes. Houses are planned, designed, and built to promote a healthier lifestyle for residents and to lower the energy footprint in our communities. This includes the materials and techniques used throughout the building process, as well as the ongoing sustainable savings applications. Green homes are a team effort: they begin with the architect and designer who initialize the concepts, and continue with the engineers and contractors who build the house.

Walls

Energy efficient walls are a basic building block of green homes. Here are the various features of the home's interior that can be energy-efficient and eco-conscious.

Aerated Autoclaved Concrete (AAC)

AAC uses a light-weight material called precast concrete. It goes through an autoclave process to get cured by steam pressure so it still insulates just like concrete.

Insulated Concrete Forms (ICF)

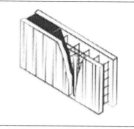	Concrete blocks (similar to large bricks) with insulation built into each block, so additional wall insulation is not needed. Rated R-17 or higher, due to their abundant thermal resistance.

Fiber Cement Siding

![siding]	Composite product constructed from wood waste reclaimed while processing. This low-maintenance product is durable (50-year warranty) and has a better fire rating than wood or metal siding.

"Green" Insulation

Made from natural or recycled materials and free from harmful unhealthy substances. Insulation is measured by its R-value (resistance to heat flow) from R-1 (weak insulation) to R-60 (better insulation) and calculated per inch. Popular green insulation materials include:

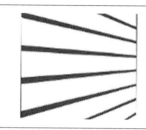	Icynene
![rigid]	Rigid Polystyrene
![aerogel]	Aerogel
![cotton]	Cotton

	Sheep's Wool

No-VOC Paint

	Paint free of Volatile Organic Compounds, which emit gas. VOC is also found in carpet, pesticides, and glue. Low-VOC and no-VOC paints are considered healthier due to higher quality air.

Straw Bale Construction

	Wheat, rye, oat, or rice straw bales used for wall structure or insulation. Sustainable because straw is a renewable product with a high insulation rating. Naturally fire retardant but does have some drawbacks.

Structure Integrated Panel (SIP)

	Insulated panels that are prefabricated at the factory, consistent across all panels. Panels are constructed of oriented strand board (OSB) on the outside, with dense foam core inside.

Trombe Wall

	Very thick masonry south-facing wall, with a glass wall in front of it. The outside wall absorbs solar heat and stores it inside the wall for gradual distribution inside.

Flooring

Sustainably harvested wood is always a good green choice. Other "GREEN" flooring includes bamboo, cork, and natural products.

Bamboo Flooring

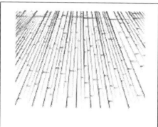	Similar to hardwood flooring, except the slats are made from bamboo stalks, which are a renewable grass plant. Color variations add natural patterns and texture. 3 types: horizontal, vertical, and strand which is compressed, then woven together. Twice as strong as oak.

Cork Flooring

	Sustainable flooring tiles made from cork trees. Has some give or "bounce" that is comfortable enough to stand on, but hard enough for a kitchen floor.

"Green" Carpet & Pad

Manufactured with reclaimed or rapidly renewable products, using non-toxic materials. Fiber carpeting without chemicals includes the following natural materials:

	Sisal
	Jute
	Wool

CRI Green Label from the Carpet Cushion Council evaluates pad emission levels, while the CRI Green Label Plus certification applies to carpet. Installation with tacks rather than glue may reduce air pollutants.

Radiant Heated Floors

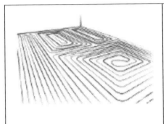 Flooring can be heated from underneath with electrical, air, or water (hydronic) systems. To install the electric method, sub-floor mats with electrical conductors are mounted under the flooring. Hydronic methods are similar. Mats with hot water tubing are underneath the tile or other flooring.

Ceilings & Attics

Solar heat enters houses through the roof and accumulates in the attic. So if you can prevent the heat, the house will stay cooler in the summer.

Attic Fan

 Roof-mounted fan that propels ventilation through the attic with an air fan. It removes the hot air and keeps the house cooler in the summer. If connected to a humidistat, it helps keep the attic dry in the winter.

Radiant Barrier Insulation

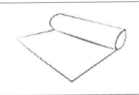 A reflective metal barrier installed in the attic, under the roof sheathing. In hot climates, it helps to reflect the sun's rays away from the house. In the winter, it prevents heat from escaping.

HVAC

Upgrading the energy efficiency of the Heating, Ventilation, and Air Conditioning (HVAC) system can be a huge step towards sustainability. Annual fuel utilization efficiency (AFUE) measures gas furnaces. Higher AFUEs indicate better efficiency. An ENERGY STAR® label means it has exceptional energy efficiency (minimum AFUE rating of 90%). We'll explore both old-fashioned methods and modern tech gadgets that conserve energy and contribute to a lower environmental impact.

Air to Air Heat Exchange

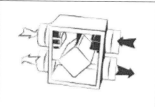

Also known as heat recovery ventilation (HRV) or mechanical ventilation heat recovery (MVHR), uses a counter-flow heat exchanger to pull in fresh air and pump stale air outside. It increases climate control while saving energy.

Co-generation Furnace

"Cogen" is a Combined Heat and Power (CHP) system that creates 2 types of energy. It generates electricity, captures the "extra" heat energy, and uses it for heating. Freewatt systems supply hot water, warm air, and electricity apart from the municipal power grid.

Enhanced Air Filtration

Efficiency and air quality can be increased simply by upgrading the media filters on HVAC equipment. For example, installing MERV filters or high level HEPA filters.

Evaporative Cooler

Cools air with water evaporation, rather than A/C equipment that uses vapor compression or refrigeration with coolant. It cools using water; not toxic coolants that deplete the ozone layer. It also provides moisture by increasing the humidity. It's "greener" because it operates more efficiently than refrigerated air conditioners and operates at 1/8 the cost. Modern evaporative coolers don't have the stigma of the previous "swamp coolers".

Ground Source Heat Pump (GSHP)

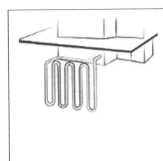

Also called "geothermal" heat, pipes installed in the ground ("ground loop") circulate liquid that absorbs the underground heat. Then it delivers that heat to the house's heating system via a heat exchanger which feeds into a heat pump. This system requires very little maintenance. Using this natural, sustainable energy could qualify residents for income or tax benefits with the government's Renewable Heat Incentive (RHI) program.

High Efficiency Furnace

A "condensing furnace" is highly efficient since it extracts more of the heat from natural gas. The heat is extracted longer, forcing the combustion exhaust gases to cool and condense. This type of furnace is considered the most energy efficient.

Windows & Lighting

The simplest, least expensive way to harness nature's power is by using windows that take advantage of the sun. Switching out light bulbs is a small but powerful strategy.

Daylighting

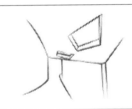

Building designed to employ sunlight through the shrewd placement of windows, openings, and reflective surfaces. Reduces energy consumption by using natural illumination rather than artificial lighting.

Low Emission Windows

Specially designed to block UV sunlight while providing energy efficiency. Protective coatings and better construction allow these dual-pane windows to absorb and reflect unwanted heat. Also known as "Low E" windows.

LED (Light-Emitting Diode) light bulb

It only takes 12 watts from an LED bulb to shine as brightly as a 60-watt incandescent. They illuminate immediately, and come in different hues. May last up to 50,000 hours and no toxic mercury to dispose of. Fit into the same light sockets, but may be heavier than other bulbs. Up to 90% energy savings from ultra-bright flood lights to dimmable room-softening lights.

CFL (Compact Fluorescent Lamp) light bulb

CFL light bulbs last about 10 times longer and burn 1/3 to 1/5 the energy of the old-fashioned incandescent light. Although they save energy, they contain toxic mercury (hazardous material) and must be responsibly recycled.

Fixtures & Appliances

Environmentally friendly appliances and fixtures are widely available and have been incorporated into the American home remodeling projects. First, let's take a look at toilet options.

Dual Flush Toilet

A toilet with two buttons for two flush options, one for liquid and another for solid waste. The button for liquid waste uses less water per flush. Becoming more popular in house remodels.

Composting Toilet

A dry toilet that processes waste without flushing water. Solid wastes are decomposed and the fumes are vented to the outside, keeping the house free of odors. Most use a compost starter and other models include foam-flush or micro-flush toilet.

Low-Flow Toilet

 A toilet that uses up to 2/3 less water than a traditional model. Newer models feature extreme water savings and are priced affordably.

Energy Star Rated Appliances

 Cut out a third of a house's energy consumption with energy efficient appliances. Every type of home appliance, lighting, water heater, fans, cooling systems, battery chargers, and electronics can be found in an ENERGY STAR rated model. Look for the label and compare!

Plumbing Systems

Reducing water and sewer usage is easy with old-fashioned low-tech methods of composting, on-site water collection, and grey water systems. Look for new tech advances with hot water heaters that qualify for tax credits and utility rebates.

On Site Water Collection

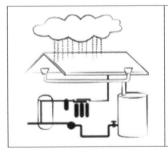 Simple wooden barrels or other containers collect rainwater from the gutter on the roof. Cisterns can be concrete, metal, fiberglass, or plastic and are sized to the roof and regional rainfall levels. This non-potable water is used for landscape irrigation. Not very successful in areas with minimal rainfall.

Grey Water System

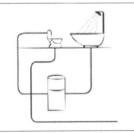 A system of recycling used water from baths, sinks, dishwashers, and clothes washers and directing it to landscaping irrigation. The same water is used twice. Also consider a whole-house plumbing system that separates water from solid waste.

Composting

Rather than flushing food scraps down the garbage disposal or in the trash, put them into a compost heap. Specially-designed containers rotate the decaying matter and turn it into vitamin-rich soil. Without proper containers, it can emit stinky odors.

Hybrid Electric Water Heater

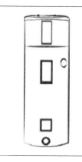

GeoSpring™ from GE is a great example of innovative technology. It absorbs heat from ambient air and pumps the heat to the water, making it 62% more efficient. While saving substantially on energy costs, it gets installed where your old water heater was, providing up to 65 gallons of hot water.

Tankless Water Heater

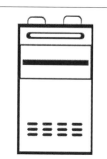

On demand water heaters produce hot water only when it's needed. It saves the cost of heating an entire tank of water around the clock. Advantages of a tankless water heater are: no lag time, and it never runs out of hot water! Two options are point-of-use heaters and whole-house heaters.

Recirculating Water Heater

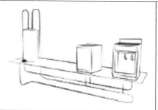

This fancy water heater prompts the system to recirculate and heat the water when it gets too cold. It activates with a timer, thermostat, motion sensor, or manually.

Electric

Handy little gadgets help control a house's energy consumption using modern technology.

Smart Thermostats

"Nest" is a state-of-the-art, easy-to-program thermostat that can offer substantial energy savings. After it "learns" your patterns, it figures out when to activate the energy-saving features. When you're away from home, you can also control the thermostat via web site or smart phone app. This smart device measures not only temperature, but also ambient light, humidity, and motion.

Motion Sensor Light Switches

Great for common area rooms, these gadgets switch on when people enter a room and automatically turn off once everyone leaves. It's smart enough to figure out when there's enough daylight so the lights don't need to come on. Can also be used with dimmers.

Load Controller

A computer mounted by the power breaker panel to measure and control the house's power usage. It prevents simultaneous high-energy usage from appliances by "load shedding" and preventing high electrical bills.

Fireplaces

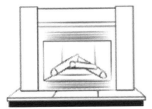

Remember the cozy feeling of sitting around the fireplace with your family on a stormy winter night? Get that same warm edge with today's amazingly energy-efficient fireplaces and stoves.

Sealed Combustion Fireplace

A direct vent fireplace pulls in fresh air from the outside of the home, as well as vents exhaust to the outside. The combustion system is sealed away from the home's living areas. This system effectively keeps the warm air inside the house and the cold air and fumes outside.

Wood-Burning Stove

The old-fashioned wood-burning stoves are making way for newer, energy efficient models approved by the EPA. They are gentler on the environment because they burn much less wood than the previous industry standard models.

Wood-Burning Stove Fireplace Insert

A large, metal, insulated stove that sits inside of a fireplace. Because it is self-contained, it keeps the temperature high and slows down the fire. It uses outside air and minimizes emissions inside the home, increasing the quality of the indoor air.

Roof

A roof can provide much more than shade and protection from elements – it can also do double duty as a garden or it can harvest energy naturally.

Living Roof

Roof planted with drought-resistant vegetation to reduce surface temperature and increase oxygen flow. Of course, the roof is coated with a water-proof membrane and features for water drainage and retention. May also provide insulation.

Passive Solar Roof

	South-facing solar panels installed on roof to capture sunlight and turn it into usable energy and/or heat. Concrete, stone, or other dense materials retain the heat until ready for use. Passive solar can minimize utility bills considerably.

Landscaping

An energy efficient home doesn't sacrifice landscaping — it can boast gorgeous curb appeal while going "green". Look for recycled materials and low water usage.

Composite Decking

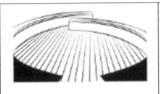	Material manufactured from plastic and/or leftover wood pieces, crafted into lumber-like slats. Used in place of hard wood, you can build a deck that is beautiful in appearance and lasts decades longer than real wood. It doesn't have to be sealed, it won't mildew or rot, and it can't get eaten by termites. Look for either hollow or solid types.

Soil Moisture Irrigation Control

	This system measures the soil moisture using sensors, and only waters when needed. Eliminates over-watering when it's rainy outside, and other drawbacks of automatic irrigation systems.

Xeriscape

	Gardens, plants, and landscaping using drought-tolerant vegetation that requires very minimal water. Substantial water savings can be realized by installing native plants in dry regions. Attracts birds and insects that are environmentally beneficial. Also known as water-conserving landscapes, drought-tolerant landscaping, and smart-scaping.

Conclusion

Now that you know all the eco-friendly features of homes, you can help your buyers shop for houses that reduce their energy bill for the long term. Arm yourself with GREEN knowledge and stand out above the crowd of competitors.

Distinguish your brand in the marketplace and establish skills in this profitable niche by getting qualified as an eco-friendly professional. Can you imagine a sustainable world where homes reflect our vibrant, healthy lifestyles? If so, you can be part of the future by showing home sellers and homeowners the benefits of going green. You can be a resource to home buyers concerned about minimizing their "footprint" on the earth, and help protect our precious natural resources.

18. Backyard & Outdoor Structures

View sample illustrations on our pinterest board:

http://www.pinterest.com/realtyproadvisr/outdoor-yard-structures

Spring welcomes the start of sunny weather, and our clients are looking for key features to enjoy the indoor/outdoor lifestyle. What's the difference between a pergola, palapa, and pavilion? Looking at a luxury home with a cabana and a crow's nest? Don't get tongue-tied... learn the lingo and be confident of your terms.

Sunshine draws home owners outside where they enjoy family barbeques and outdoor entertaining. Want to brush on the terms before meeting your client? Here's our all-seasons guide to the industry jargon you'll need to know when navigating back yards.

Arbor

	A wooden or metal arched structure. The sides incorporate trellis-work lattice with green vines or climbing shrubs. For durability and lower cost, vinyl may be substituted for the wood construction.
	Outdoor weddings often include beautifully decorated arbors, which the bride and groom walk through or stand under.

Balcony

	A decorative platform that protrudes from an upper story of a building. Railing is often black wrought iron. Balconies range in size – they can be very tiny or large enough for outdoor patio furniture.
	Decorative styles add character to the home and reflect the culture and architectural period. For example: Italian, Greek, or Spanish.
	A Juliet balcony, named after Romeo & Juliet fame, is a balcony that does not protrude from the building.

Cabana

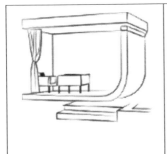

An outdoor room with curtains or drapes, commonly used to lounge near a swimming pool or beach.

It may have a solid wall or may be a transportable structure. The drapes close to provide shelter from the sun and wind.

A cabana may also be a tent-like structure; or in tropical climates, it may have a thatched roof.

Cabana Pool House

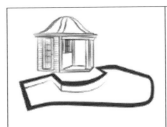

A cabana pool house is a freestanding enclosed room used as a bathhouse or for relaxing near the pool. It is a permanent structure and so it provides more protection from the wind and sun than a curtain or tent cabana.

With many windows and lots of sunlight, it's similar to an enclosed porch. Also known as a cabana room.

Crow's Nest

A small deck on top of a roof that perches above the house for an aerial view. The deck is accessed via stairs from inside the house. Crows nests are often seen in luxury homes near vantage viewpoints; for example near the ocean or a lake.

Originally a crow's nest referred to a lookout point on the main mast of a ship. Also known as a rooftop deck or a lookout.

Courtyard

A patio on the interior of a home, which is enclosed by building walls. It is unroofed and open to the sky. This indoor/outdoor living space warm climates is often planted with trees, shrubs, flowers, and other greenery.

Courtyards are popular in Spanish style homes, tropical areas, housing complexes, castles, and large office buildings. Also known as a court or an interior courtyard.

Deck

A platform structure with no roof that is attached to a house or other building. It may have a railing around it. Typically located right outside the back door or the back stairs, but in metro areas may be on a rooftop.

Decks are typically built with solid wood, which eventually decays. Building materials include: solid wood (redwood, cedar, pine), composite decking made from recycled wood fibers, or synthetic decking made of artificial wood. Trex is a popular artificial lumber that lasts longer than solid wood. It's gaining in popularity because it doesn't rot or mold, and it's not a haven for termites who like solid wood.

Gazebo

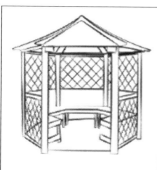

A free-standing round or square wooden structure with a platform and a roof. It may have side railings, drapes, or lattice. The roof can be a cloth or vinyl canopy with mesh screen sides or open sides, such as a portable structure.

The platform is often slightly elevated to provide an attractive view of the beautiful surrounding gardens. Gazebos are popular garden and back yard structures and sometimes have a hot tub inside.

AKA summerhouse, sun canopy, open or latticework pavilion, pagoda (Asian style).

Lanai

An outdoor patio room attached to the house and used as living quarters in warm, tropical climates. The room has a roof and may be partially sided or have a railing. It may have screens or large picture windows, or may be open. It is furnished with rattan living and dining room furniture, since alfresco dining is the tradition in tropical areas.

Lanais are most common in topical locations such as Hawaii and Florida.

Palapa

An outdoor shade structure with a thatched roof and open sides. Since this is a tropical design, the roof is constructed from palm tree leaves.

Palapas started as small umbrella-like structures, but in luxury homes they often encompass an open building. For example, it may house a backyard barbeque pit and outdoor kitchen. Also known as a tiki hut or grass hut. Palapa also refers to a beach umbrella with a thatched leaf top.

Patio

A platform improvement in a back yard or garden, made with concrete, brick, or stone, rock, or flagstone. It is adjacent to the home, usually accessible from sliding glass doors inside the home.

A patio may be covered, but often is completely open. It's known as a place where families can gather together for outdoor living and summertime fun together.

Pavilion

A small ornamental roofed building in a yard or a garden. The living space has no walls but is furnished for outdoor entertainment.

Large pavilions are often located in public place, but smaller pavilions are designed for back yards too. They are popular in southern and older style properties.

Pergola

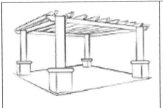

A free-standing rectangular structure with pillars or support columns and wooden slats running across the top. Lattice often provides a partially shaded top so the pergola can be used as a walkway or sitting area.

The columns and slats are often intertwined with green vines and climbing plants, making a graceful garden feature.

Porch / Enclosed porch

An outdoor deck attached to a house that aligns with the front entry to the house, shaded by the house roof.

An enclosed porch is closed in with windows or screens, letting in breezes and sunlight.

Stoop

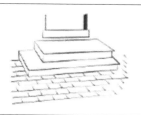

A small block of cement on the ground as a step-out of a building. A stoop can be as small as 2' x 2'.

To save money, new home developers often pour a small concrete stoop outside the back door, rather than a patio.

Sunroom

A sunny all-seasons porch on the side of a house, enclosed with large windows. A sunroom provides some shelter from the weather while catching maximum sunlight.

Also referred to as a patio room, solarium, conservatory, Florida room, or California room (depending on the region).

Terrace

Similar to a patio but larger and more developed, a terrace is a platform that extends from a home and is used as an outdoor living area. In luxury homes, a terrace may showcase formal gardens and upscale features such as statues.

In New York and metro areas, an apartment may have a terrace on an upper floor or even on the roof!

Veranda

 A large roofed porch that wraps around the sides and front of a house. A veranda has railing and is most common in the warm South, where families would sit outside during the summer (before air conditioning was invented).

This type of outdoor structure is often found in colonial style, plantation style, and Victorian style homes. Sometimes larger farmhouse style homes may also boast a veranda.

A veranda may also refer to an enclosed porch or a sunroom. AKA terms: portico, gallery, piazza.

Conclusion

Who knew there were so many outdoor types of structures? When showing a property, now you can explain the difference between arbors and pergolas, gazebos and verandas. Brush up on these garden terms and you will surely impress your clients. Your skills will shine as you prepare for spring selling season!

19. Fences and Gates

View sample illustrations on our pinterest board:

http://www.pinterest.com/realtyproadvisr/fences-gates

Open the gates to a wonderful home for your buyer clients! Does their ideal dream home include a "white picket fence" in the front yard? A gorgeous entry gate can be a beautiful bonus for your new home owners.

Fences are used to define property boundaries (even though land surveys show they are often placed incorrectly). Fences also protect gardens, keep dogs or horses enclosed, ensure swimming pool safety, scare away intruders, and beautify a yard.

A gate is simply an entryway in a fence, or a swinging door that opens into a yard. Gates are made from the same materials as fences, and installed with hinges or an opening mechanism. They may be adorned with fancy pillars or hand-carved posts. A Hampshire gate is a thin-wire gate on a farm that can be twisted away from the fence.

Fence & Gate Styles

In a property listing, you may see a "good neighbor fence" in a tract home or "cross fencing" out in the country. We often see retaining walls terracing a hillside. And if you've been out on a ranch, you've probably seen cattle gates in conjunction with cattle guards – metal grids across the road designed to prevent cows from crossing.

Arched (Concave)

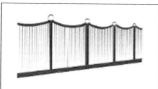 When the fence sections fan downwards (concave) between posts. Many types of fence tops / finishes can be rounded or arched.

Arched (Convex)

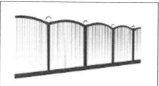 When the fence sections fan upwards (convex) between posts.

Board on Board

Overlapping vertical boards without spacing. Expensive to build but ensures maximum privacy.

Board to Board

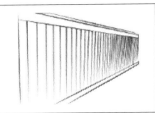

Vertical wooden boards butted together without spacing, so there is no visibility.

Capped

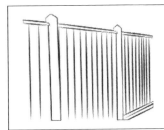

Decorative tops installed in various patterns on posts or boards.

Corral

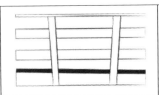

Designed for livestock, boards are installed horizontally and spaced out, meeting at posts. Boards can be logs, tree branches, or reused slats. Economical design for ranches and farms.

Dog Eared Top

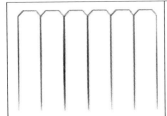

The top of each board (picket) is cut off on an angle on each side. Very traditional style and used commonly.

Gothic Top

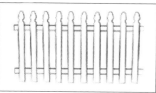
The top of each rod or board culminates in a sharp, decorative point.

Good Neighbor

Sections of fence alternate front and back during the length of the fence, so that each neighbor has some front-facing and back-facing sections.

Horse

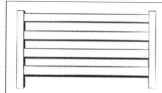
Specially designed for horses, it flexes for safety.

Lattice or Lattice Top

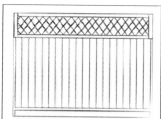
Wood or vinyl material in a see-through diamond pattern.

Picket

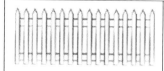
Thin wood or vinyl boards are spaced apart and the tops are pointed. Usually a low type of fence designed for style.

Picket Top

	A decorative style of spaced boards at the top of a regular wooden fence.

Scalloped

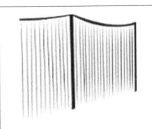	Arched design that curves up or down. Opposite of a flat top. Refer to "Arched" above.

Shadow Board or Shadowbox

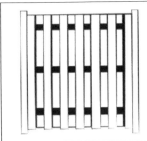	Staggered boards, alternating front and back, allow slight visibility between the boards (pickets). Often used as a good neighbor fence because both neighbors get an equal share of front & back.

Split Rail

	Similar to a corral fence, boards are horizontal. Often installed in a zig-zag pattern that allows ranchers to quickly calculate the length of the area covered.

Fencing Materials

Popular fencing materials include wood, artificial materials, metal, natural materials, and safety / protective fences.

Wood

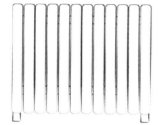

Natural material made from trees with a wide variety of styles and finishes. Wood will warp, fade, and rot, unless finished with stain or paint and a protective gloss. Specially treated wood can reduce termite pest invasion caused by water damage. Popular woods include:

- Oak
- Pine
- Redwood
- Fir
- Cedar
- Spruce

Artificial Materials

Vinyl – synthetic materials can be custom designed and factory ordered to imitate wood, stone, or wrought iron. Extremely durable material that will neither rust like metal, nor rot like wood.

Composite – wood-look "sleeves" created with recycled materials and installed with wood posts. "Green" sustainable composite also available.

Metal

Wrought Iron – ornamental black iron welded into scrolls and other elegant designs.

Steel – vertical metal rails add stylish design while allowing light and visibility.

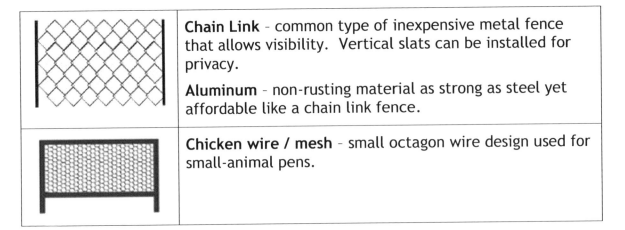

	Chain Link – common type of inexpensive metal fence that allows visibility. Vertical slats can be installed for privacy. **Aluminum** – non-rusting material as strong as steel yet affordable like a chain link fence.
	Chicken wire / mesh – small octagon wire design used for small-animal pens.

Natural Materials

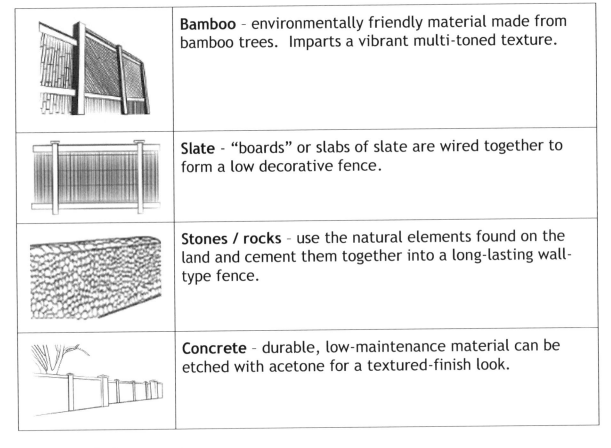

	Bamboo – environmentally friendly material made from bamboo trees. Imparts a vibrant multi-toned texture.
	Slate – "boards" or slabs of slate are wired together to form a low decorative fence.
	Stones / rocks – use the natural elements found on the land and cement them together into a long-lasting wall-type fence.
	Concrete – durable, low-maintenance material can be etched with acetone for a textured-finish look.

Safety / Protective

Fences designed to keep people (or animals) in or out, safety fences can be metal or even invisible.

Barbed Wire

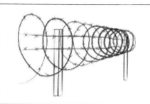

	Steel wires with prickly metal barbs at regular intervals to discourage people or livestock from crossing.

Electrical Fence

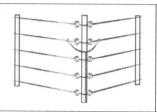

	Metal wires transmit an electric shock when touched; meant to keep animals from crossing.

Invisible Fence

	An electrical wire that lays on (or under) the ground, forming a fence line. The goal is to keep pets from crossing the perimeter of the property.

Conclusion

Elements can be combined to create attractive fences and gates which lend appeal to your listing! Environmentally friendly fences reuse and recycle old wood. "Fences create good neighbors," as the saying goes, but fences also provide privacy, ensure safety, and create eye-catching curb appeal.

Privacy fence or perimeter fence? Now you know the difference! Equipped with gate and fence lingo, you can easily describe them to your clients. Get familiar with fence materials and find out about styles so you can find the perfect home for your buyers And you can now identify various styles, materials, and usages. You're the gate and fence expert!

20. Rural Properties

View sample illustrations on our pinterest board:

http://www.pinterest.com/realtyproadvisr/rural-properties

Do you love the country? Green rolling hills, giant trees, animals roaming, crops thriving, and breath-taking starry skies at night amidst peace and quiet. If so, consider specializing in selling rural property. Your clients will be motivated by your zeal for the country lifestyle.

Whether you have buyers looking for a hobby farm, an equestrian estate, a vineyard, a self-sustaining family compound "off the grid", or a simple homestead, rural properties are both challenging and thrilling to sell. Architectural styles range from rustic ranches to custom castles, log cabins to custom Mediterranean, buried eco-conscious walls to manufactured homes to elaborate gentleman estates — every home is unique.

Some buyers move out to the country to raise their family with a slower pace of life, living a short drive away from the city. Home buyers move from the city to the country to enjoy the privacy and isolation. Life is calmer without light pollution or noisy neighbors.

Rural property owners may want to live in peace and quiet away from city noise. The acreage isn't always about having the most land, but is often about privacy. Neighbors seem distant and solitude is valued. The open space is a bonus for those holding large family gatherings or buyers bringing their dirt bikes and quads for racing!

Rural property can be less expensive if it's far out in the "boonies", but remember it won't be valued at price per square foot of the house, like regular residential property. Perhaps your buyers need a place to store an inventory of classic cars, or work on their hobby. Maybe they want to relocate their entire family together, or just be closer to nature and live off the land.

Variety abounds because no two properties are alike. In addition, you'll become familiar with unique aspects of rural properties. Let's discuss sustainable utilities.

Sustainable Utilities

Have you ever seen an electrical meter that runs backwards? The home owners are generating power and selling it to the power company, instead of buying it. You'll learn the 2 types of creeks: those you can see, and underground creeks you cannot see. You discover septic tanks (hold your nose when it's being pumped out), propane tanks (remember the on/off switch), water wells (they need power to operate), leach fields, and natural wind / solar power.

Water

Water levels are different on each property, so digging a well may be simple or more complex, depending on the water level depth, and how much rocky soil is above it. Note to your buyers: the cost of digging a well depends on how deep they must drill to find the water level. Often, buyers will want to locate water sources as part of their due diligence investigation before purchasing.

 **Drilled water wells** consist of pipes driven into the ground until they reach the groundwater table, then water pumped up to the surface. Other types are dug wells and driven wells for more shallow water tables. Well water must be tested regularly for bacteria and the quality must be maintained due to possible contamination.

Gone is the old-fashioned method of lowering a bucket into an open well.

 **Creeks** are a good source of water, although not always reliable year-round. Fresh running water is available after a rainy season, or when snow melts on the mountains above. Note that neighbors may block or pollute creeks on their property, which would affect other properties downstream.

 **Rainwater collection** is a sustainable method of harvesting clean water by collecting it in barrels. Rain from rooftops can easily be routed into the collection system and stored for garden irrigation later. Although it won't supply all of the home's water needs, it can certainly help conserve home water usage.

Fuel

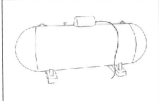 **Propane tanks** are the ranch's answer to a sustainable fuel source. Those giant metal tanks are seen near the house and supply propane instead of gas. Home owners contract with a propane company that fills the tank regularly. Creative country dwellers have even painted their propane tanks to turn those ugly metal creatures into cute and crazy features.

Energy

	Old-style **wooden windmills** have been exchanged for modern wind turbines that generate energy from the air flow, a renewable energy source, and convert it to electricity.
	Tech advances helped create vertical **wind turbines**, effective for home use. Small, residential wind power systems are installed as towers atop large properties.
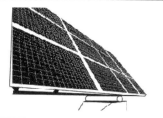	**Solar panels**, either on top of the house or spread throughout the property, are often seen in rural properties. Solar power is the most common type of renewable energy. The panels capture sunlight with photovoltaic cells and turn it into electricity.
	**Geothermal energy** taps the earth's thermal energy by collecting energy under the ground and pumping it into the house. It comes into the heat exchanger system and then can be used to heat or cool the house.
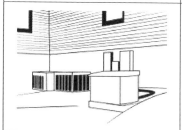	A **power generator** requires fuel, such as gasoline or propane, to operate. In an emergency, it can power an entire house. For more self-sustaining energy sources, refer to our article on "Green" energy.

Waste Disposal

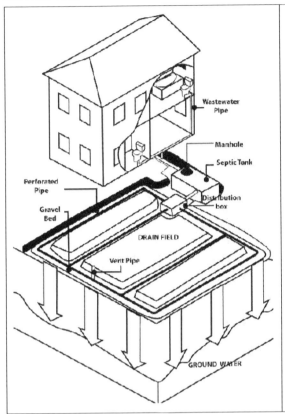

A **septic system** removes wastewater from the house through the plumbing pipes, just like a sewer system, except that the waste remains on the property. It flows into a septic tank in the back yard where the solid waste accumulates and gets pumped out every few years. It can be treated with chemical and organic compounds to minimize the odor and build-up.

A septic tank inspection, which buyers usually request, will require the tank to be emptied. As an agent, you can usually identify the location of the drain field (also known as leach field or absorption field) because of the tall, green grass growing on top of it.

Before recycling, there was recycling. It's what people did years ago before landfills. Today, rural homeowners sort their trash, dispose of it accordingly, and then recycle the rest. For example: paper gets burned in the fireplace; edible food scraps get fed to the animals, inedible food waste goes in the compost pile; and plastics get recycled, reused, or repurposed.

Occasionally home owners will burn trash in a barrel, a pile, or an outdoor boiler. Burning trash is a last resort, because even if it is allowed in rural areas, it creates thick smoke that may be toxic. Hopefully, those sellers will have hauled their trash into a landfill instead of letting it build up or burning it. Watch out for abandoned trash which becomes an eyesore on the property.

Communication

On rural properties, landline phones may be the only form of telephone communication when mobile phones do not receive a reliable signal. Unless you drive up to the top of a hill — then you're bound to hear it crystal clear.

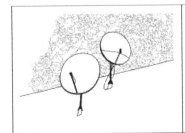

With the advent of **small satellite dishes**, rural residents can receive both TV and internet reception (although it may be spotty at times). For those work-from-home business folks, slow or low-speed internet may not be sufficient and they may have to upgrade with a powerful antenna.

Land Usage

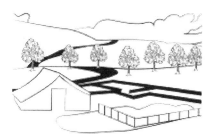

Rural property can be utilized in various ways and for diverse purposes. The maximum "highest and best" usage depends up on the zoning classification, either from the local city or the county (which has jurisdiction in unincorporated areas).

Zoning

Rural property may be zoned as rural, agricultural, open space, rural residential, or a similar designation. When taking a listing, agents are advised to research the zoning to ascertain potential uses, so they can market to the widest pool of buyers.

In some areas, tax laws may favor and seek to protect rural land, such as the Williamson Act in California. Properties protected under this Act benefit from extremely low tax rates, provided that they do not develop the property further.

Developing

Rural property buyers who want to create a family compound for multiple generations to live together often prefer to develop the property after purchase. Buyers should research the county zoning and watch out for unexpected downgrades. In addition, building permits may be challenging to get approved. Existing structures are valuable, even if run-down, because it may be difficult to obtain building permits for new structures.

Other considerations for buyers include government-required allocation of dedicated open space, hill slope usability, entitlements in place, and ingress/egress easements from neighbors. Buyer will discover this information when performing their due diligence research before purchase.

Crops

One of the many benefits of rural properties is that home owners can grow their own produce. Besides the value of harvesting a home-grown garden full of organic vegetables and fruits, homeowners can compost organic waste into the next crop's nutrients. Nets and shields are often used to deflect pests such as bugs and birds. Fences are built to keep out animals such as deer and squirrels.

Buyers may want to purchase rural property for agricultural uses. Crops, orchards, and vineyards are commercial applications of acreage. Each of these uses have their own specific requirements for soil, water source, irrigation, land slope, and sunlight exposure. Agents representing ag buyers will be familiar with these requests. Expect to see heavy equipment such as tractors and farming supplies.

Equestrian

Many horse lovers dream of buying their perfect horse ranch, known as an equestrian property. They may train race horses, groom show horses, or simply enjoy riding horses. Some even care for rescued horses. The acreage includes space for a corral, a tack barn (to house food and supplies), and riding trails.

Farm Animals

Most rural property owners enjoy animals as part of their lifestyle, including pets. Ranchers raise farm animals, either individually or commercially. Common farm animals include cows, goats, chickens, and pigs. Animal products include farm-fresh eggs, unpasteurized milk, and eventually, meat (slaughtered for food).

The property will include facilities to feed, house, and care for the animals, as well as processing plants and equipment. Although illegal, rural properties have been known to include chicken coops for cock fighting, an age-old country pastime. Savvy agents will recognize the coops right away.

Expect the property to be fenced and cross-fenced so animals don't escape. The first thing buyers will notice about farm animal property is the pungent manure smell, although they will eventually get used to it.

Buildings

Although buildings require permits to be "legal", rural properties are known for sheds, outhouses, unpermitted structures, and DIY "add-ons". Agents advertising rural listings must be careful to discern and advertise as habitable only those buildings known to be permitted. Rural property buyers usually understand that "what they see is what they get" and it's part of the appeal of country living.

Junk

With no neighbors for miles around, some country dwellers have been known to collect loads of junk on the property. After years of collecting "stuff", debris removal can be a substantial challenge for a listing agent. Rural areas may not be policed except after neighbor complaints, which fosters issues such as junk pile-ups, illegal crops, and accumulation of weird stuff on the property. County regulations may not be heavily enforced so the term "buyer beware" certainly applies.

Showing & Selling

Rural property is fun to show and sell as you get to explore interesting facets of each piece of land. But viewing a couple of rural properties can take an entire day. After a one or two hour drive to get there, viewing them can be very extensive and exhausting.

Navigation

Surprisingly different from showing tract houses, listing agents will prepare in advance with a GPS navigation system and a Thomas Guide map back-up. Due to the many unpaved dirt roads and private unnamed streets, it's embarrassingly easy to get lost with clients in tow. Don't depend on your phone navigation system, as you may not get reception. Plan ahead and get detailed directions from the listing agent in advance. You may encounter steep winding roads, difficult terrain that requires 4-wheel drive vehicles, and stubborn cows that won't move out of the middle of the road.

Walking the Property

When initially taking a listing, the first thing agents do is walk the property with the seller to identify the property boundaries. Wear your boots and be prepared for hiking slopes, climbing fences, and splashing through creeks. Be sure to avoid gopher holes, poison oak, cow patties, and other hazards. Bring a compass to navigate. Don't depend solely upon your cell phone as the reception may be non-existent or it may run out of battery.

Maps & Boundaries

As a listing agent becoming familiar with your listing, or as a buyer's agent performing your due diligence, you'll analyze many types of maps: topo (topographical) maps (with hills marked), plat maps from the county, and aerial photos and maps. If the property was sub-divided in an unusual shape, as often happens with acreage, boundary lines may be difficult to determine. Some borders may be fenced, others left unfenced, and still others the fence is not along the correct boundary.

Title

When reading the title report, agents may see property boundaries with creative metes and bounds title descriptions, such as "the large rock by the oak tree two feet from the northwest end of the creek" rather than standard lot, block, and tract descriptions. The buyer will want to hire a land surveyor if they need to determine the exact boundaries.

Vendors

Some of the many specialized vendors for rural properties include:

- Geological / soils engineer - to test soil for minerals and agricultural planting.
- County building & planning dept. (to find out how many/how large residences can be built on the land).
- Well drilling company - get an estimate of the cost to drill a new well, and measure the number of feet down to access the water table
- State water commission - to find out where the creek beds are, and if there are any protected animal species in the creek.
- County zoning dept. - to find out if zoning RR (rural residence) means 2 houses or 3; and what are future plans for the area?
- California Coastal commission - to find out about building height of properties facing the ocean, or viewable from the ocean - or if you can even build at all!
- Orchard analyst - to determine if crops will grow on that northeast patch of land - and what type of irrigation is needed.
- Land surveyor - to mark the property lot lines (for your client's peace of mind) - there may NOT be any fences around the property boundaries -- and the fences are often wrong anyway.

Conclusion

Whether it's a custom castle on acreage, an equestrian estate, or a tiny home on a ranch off the grid, rural property is a unique niche for agents who love the country lifestyle. In last month's article, we discovered utilities on rural property. This time we explore land usage, and most importantly the nuances of showing and selling rural property.

Now that you know all about rural property, you can advise your sellers and advertise your listings to sell for top dollar. As an experienced agent, you discovered how to start researching properties for your buyers. A few other purchase considerations for your buyer include fire insurance rates, the new state parcel tax fee (for fire protection), condition of the wells, and future cost of private road maintenance. Here's to your success as a rural property agent!

APPENDIX

Our appendix includes a glossary of real estate transaction terms and a chart with definitions for commonly used acronyms.

Glossary of Transaction Terms

This glossary, written specifically for home buyers, is pulled from my book, "Buy Your First Home: A Basic Step-by-Step Guide for First Time Home Buyers."

<u>Terms & Definitions</u> are explained in simple, easy-to-understand words. These are not legal definitions. They are the author's opinion based on her knowledge and experience.

100% Financing	A mortgage loan that does not require a down payment from the payment (does not mean that closing costs are waived or paid).
1031 Exchange	A technique of selling one property without having to pay current capital gains taxes because the seller is simultaneously acquiring another property.
Additional Principal Payments	Additional money that a homeowner (borrower) pays to reduce their mortgage balance due.
Amenities	Valuable items included in a house purchase, and could be part of the community also, such as an HOA swimming pool.
American Dream	The admired ideals of freedom as embodied by the culture of the United States of America.
Appliances	Large electronic items often included with sale of a house. For example: stove/oven/range, dishwasher, refrigerator, clothes washer and dryer, micro-hood.
Appraisal	A written report by a licensed appraiser, including an opinion of a house's value.
Appreciation	The amount of value that a property has increased.

Approval Letter	Letter from a mortgage lender that includes a commitment to loan you an exact amount of money, on a specific house, with a specific closing date. It states the interest rate and payment amounts.
Approved	Buyer who has received an approval letter from his/her mortgage lender.
Assets	Items of value that you own.
Attorney Closing	An escrow/settlement process in a state that utilizes attorneys instead of escrow companies. States that requires an attorney for deed preparation include FL, GA, IL, KY, LA, MD, MA, MI, NJ, NY, NC, OH, OR, SC, TX, VA, WA, DC, WV.
Back End Ratio	Your "front end" housing payment PLUS all your monthly consumer debts.
Backup Offer / Backup Position	An offer that is submitted to a seller already under contract, just in case the current buyer backs up.
Backup Plan (AKA Plan B)	An alternative strategy that you will take, if your 1st strategy doesn't work out.
Bidding Process	Home buyers who are all competing for the same house at the same time.
Budget	A spreadsheet that calculates a family's income, expenses, & savings.
Buyer Representation Agreement (BRA or BRE)	A contract to hire a buyer's agent. Sometimes called a **Buyer Broker Agreement.**
Cash Reserves	Money in an account which can be liquefied (withdrawn) if needed.
Certified Funds	A money order or a cashier's check issued by a credible bank.
Closing Attorney	Closing attorneys are required to direct the closing process in some states. States that requires an attorney for deed preparation include FL, GA, IL, KY, LA, MD, MA, MI, NJ, NY, NC, OH, OR, SC, TX, VA, WA, DC, WV.

Closing Costs	The fees charged to buyers and sellers that are paid as part of the cost of the transaction.
Closing Period (AKA Escrow Period Or Settlement Period)	The time frame of the transaction purchase finalizing.
Community Property	Property that is owned jointly by husband and wife, even if both of their names are not on the legal title.
Competitive Offer	Purchase offer which has a high price and good terms, backed by a solid, qualified buyer.
Comps / Comparable	Houses that are in a similar neighborhood, and are similar sizes, and were built around the same time period, are called "comparable" because they can be compared to each other.
Concessions	Credits or favorable monetary terms extended from the seller to the buyer.
Condo / Condominium	A housing project with attached walls, where each homeowner owns their own unit.
Consumer Debt	Any credit account you used to buy electronic goods, household furniture, take vacations, buy clothing and jewelry, and spend for Christmas presents or anything that is not considered an appreciating asset.
Consummated	Officially started or began something, such as a contract going into effect.
Contingency (AKA Subject To)	Certain conditions that must be fulfilled in order for the purchase to proceed.
Contingency Period	The time frame in which conditions are fulfilled before the purchase contract is in full effect and can proceed.
Conventional Loan	A mortgage loan that is NOT issued or insured by a government agency, such as Fannie Mae or HUD.
Convey	Items that will be staying with the property upon sale because they are included with the purchase of the house.

Co-Payment	A small, flat fee that a homeowner pays in lieu of the entire cost of a repair. With a home warranty.
Co-Sign	When a buyer/borrower is not strongly qualified, a co-signer is an additional person who signs on the loan as a guarantor.
Counter Offer	An acceptance of an offer, but with some changes.
Credit Bureau	1 of the 3 major companies that sells credit reports & credit scores.
Credit Counselor	A professional who assists consumers to lower their debt by paying off credit accounts and challenging inaccurate credit entries.
Credit Scores	FICO scores from 3 consumer credit reports, rating each consumer's credit-worthiness and the likelihood they will repay their debts on time.
Crime Statistics	Calculations about various types of crimes in a neighborhood or city.
Customary Split	The responsibility for paying standard fees, which are typical for your region.
Debt Consolidation	The process of taking several debts and combining them all into 1 single, smaller payment.
Debt Ratio	These debts are measured against your monthly income and calculated as a ratio.
Debt-Free	A lifestyle choice of living without owning anyone any money.
Decision-Makers	People who have a vested interest in a transaction and the ability to influence the parties (buyers & sellers).
Deductible	When an insurance claim is filed, the deductible is the amount of money that the policy holder must pay before insurance begins paying its share.

Delayed Gratification	The concept of waiting until later to purchase things.
Demographic Data	Info by zip codes, such as the average income of a household, the educational level, and number of people in a family.
Depreciation	The amount of value that a property has decreased.
Disclosures	Documents that communicate important info from one party to another or document the condition of the house. Some are required as legal disclaimers.
Disposable Income	The "extra" cash that is left over from your paycheck after you have paid all your necessary bills.
Downpayment (AKA "Down Payment")	The total amount of cash that home buyer is putting down (not including closing costs) usually expressed as a certain % of the purchase price.
Due Diligence	The process of investigating all of the features about a house to verify its condition. It is the buyers' responsibility to do their "due diligence" research before purchasing.
Earnest Money Deposit (EMD)	The check that the buyer writes as the initial down payment and submits with their purchase offer.
Electronic Signature (AKA e-Signature)	A digital signature applied to disc online or via a tech gadget.
Equity	The amount of ownership that you have in your house, over and above the amount you owe on the mortgage loan.
Escrow	The process of administering a real estate sales transaction. A neutral party to facilitate the money and the transaction between buyer and seller.

Escrow Company (AKA Settlement Company, depending on the state)	The entity that holds the buyer's earnest money deposit while processing the transaction sale. In some areas, the title company also acts as the escrow company.
Escrow Officer (AKA Settlement Officer, depending on the state)	An escrow company employee who is responsible for closing a transaction.
Escrow Funds (AKA Reserve Funds)	Money that the mortgage lender collects in addition to the mortgage payment. The additional funds are put into an impound account (AKA escrow account) and used to pay the borrower's property taxes and homeowners insurance.
Established Neighborhood	A community that is more mature because it's been in existence for many years.
Estimated Closing Statement (AKA Settlement Statement)	The HUD-1 or the escrow company calculation that shows a breakdown of buyer/seller credits and debits for closing.
FICO Score	Refer to "credit scores".
Financial Habits	Putting into place a continuous system of good money management.
Financial Planner	A licensed professional who can assist you in reaching your family's goals. A certified or licensed business professional that helps families manages their finances wisely, grow wealth, and protect assets.
Floor Plan	Diagram of a house's layout, including a sketch of the rooms.
Free & Clear	Owning a home with no mortgage or liens against it.
Front End Ratio	Your total housing payment, including mortgage, PMI, property taxes, & insurance.
Good Money Management	The practice of accounting for income and expenses and overseeing it well.

Home Inspection (AKA Structural Building Inspection)	A structural inspection of the house by an experienced professional. The inspector will write a report stating the results of the inspection.
Home Warranty	A prepaid annual policy that guarantees broken items in the house will be fixed with only a small co-payment. The home warranty company will fix things when they break, with only a small co-payment due from the home owner. Similar to an insurance policy.
Homeowner	A person who owns the house they live in, with his/her name legally on title.
HomeOwner Association (HOA)	The association that makes rules for a neighborhood, collects monthly fees, and pays common-area expenses. HOA fees are mandatory if the home is in an HOA area.
Homeowners Insurance (AKA Fire Insurance or Hazard Insurance)	Insurance that protects the house by guaranteeing that the homeowners will be compensated in case of a loss. The insurance company pays for broken/burned real property which was covered in the policy.
Impound Account	Along with your mortgage payment each month, you pay additional money ("Escrow Reserves") to cover the cost of the property taxes and homeowners insurance. The mortgage company puts this money into an impound account, and then pays the insurance and taxes every year so the homeowner doesn't have to worry about paying it annually as a lump sum.
Instant Email Alerts	Newly listed houses for sale that are sent to home buyers.
Insurance Policy	A contract between a home owner and the insurance company that determines the claims which the company will cover.
Itemized Deductions	Expenses and credits that can be subtracted from the tax payer's 1040 tax return. Compare to standard deductions.

Legacy	Something that you create, either tangible or intangible, from which future generations will benefit.
Legal Obligation	Something you are committed to do because it is a law or because you have signed a written, legally binding contract.
Legal Service Plan	A membership-based business service that offers legal advice from attorneys to members at a low monthly cost. An example is LegalShield®.
Life Insurance	A written insurance policy that pays money to your dependents upon your death or permanent disability.
Life Span	The number of years an appliance (or home improvement) will typically last.
List Price (AKA Asking Price)	The amount of a seller markets his house that (not the same as value).
Living Trust (AKA Family Living Trust)	A legal entity formed for the purpose of protecting assets, such as real property.
Mello-Roos Fees	A common assessment (fee) in California which is billed to home owners.
Mortgage Insurance (AKA "PMI")	Mortgage insurance is required by mortgage lenders when you don't have a large enough downpayment (typically less than 20%). It protects the lender by covering losses they may incur if you default on your loan.
Mortgage Loan	A loan for debt which is secured against the house.
Move-Up Home	A house purchased by existing homeowners who are moving up to a bigger or better home. Compare to "Starter Home".
Mutual Agreement of Both Parties	The seller and buyer have both agreed upon the price and terms.
Negotiable	An item that is subject to discussion between the parties.

Negotiation Process	When the buyer and seller are discussing what each party will give and take.
Neighborhood Blight	Conditions that de-value a community.
Nest Egg	Money that is put aside for retirement and future planning.
Notary Public	A person commission by the State who is present to notarize your signature on legal documents, such as the mortgage loan documents.
Offer / Purchase Offer / Offer to Purchase (AKA Bid)	A document from a buyer to a seller to purchase.
Open Escrow	Process of a neutral party (escrow company) starting to process a sale transaction after all parties have executed (signed) the contract.
Overlap Occupancy	Having possession of 2 houses to enable you to move out of 1 house and into another easily.
Owner-Occupant Buyers	Families who will live in the home they buy.
Personal Property	Items which are not real property and not included in the home purchase.
Pest Control Inspection (AKA Termite Inspection)	An inspection to check the building's structural integrity due to possible damage by termites (wood-destroying pests) or water. The report is divided into Sections 1 and 2. Most mortgage lenders will require a Certificate of Clearance for Section 1.
Planned Unit Development (PUD)	A housing project where each homeowner owns a part of the common areas and the entire community is governed by rules.
Preliminary Title Report (AKA "Prelim")	A search of the legal ownership of a house and any liens against it, or other challenges to the legal title.
Pre-Payment Penalty	A large lump sum of money which a borrower must pay to their mortgage lender in order to pay off their mortgage early.

Pre-Qualification Letter	Letter from a mortgage lender that includes the dollar amount for which you are qualified to show for houses. It's an unofficial estimate and is not highly regarded for accuracy.
Pre-Qualified	Buyer who has received a pre-qualification letter from his/her mortgage lender.
Preventive Maintenance	The process of keeping the house repaired and maintained on a regular basis to lessen the change of major repair crises.
Price Range	A dollar amount that varies from a low amount to high amount.
Principal	The amount of money borrowed on your mortgage loan that must be paid back.
Property Taxes	A real estate tax assessed & collected by the county, based on the value of the property.
Purchase Contract (AKA Sales Contract)	An agreement between a buyer and a seller of a house for sale.
Qualification Letter	Letter from a mortgage lender that includes desktop underwriting (DU) approval stating how much money you can borrow and the interest rate of the loan.
Qualified	Buyer who has received a qualification letter from his/her mortgage lender.
Ratified Contract (AKA Fully Executed)	Document signed by all parties to make it a legal agreement.
REALTOR®	A real estate agent who is a member of the National Association of Realtors®.
Recorded Deed	The Deed of Trust (AKA warranty deed) officially and legally transfer to new owner recorded at the county clerk- recorder's office, which then becomes a publicly recorded document.
REO (AKA Bank Owned)	House which is owned by the mortgage lender that foreclosed on the house.

Repair Request	The buyer can request that the seller to either: fix the broken items, give a repair credit, or lower the purchase price to compensate for the broken items.
Search Criteria	Items that buyers categorize to help them find houses that meet their families' needs, such as list price, zip codes, and number of bedrooms.
Seasoned Funds	Money that has been sitting in the buyer's bank account for a certain number of months (usually 2 months).
Service Call	The cost for a contractor to visit the house and inspect or fix repairs.
Settlement Company (AKA Escrow Company, depending on the state)	The entity that holds the buyer's earnest money deposit while processing the transaction sale.
Settlement Officer (AKA Escrow Officer, depending the state)	A settlement company employee who is responsible for closing a transaction.
Short Sale	Sale of a house which has a higher mortgage than the value of the house, therefore the mortgage lender must approve the sale.
Sign Off on Contract (AKA Remove All Contingencies)	Buyer agrees to proceed with finalizing the purchase, and now cannot back out without a penalty.
Single Family Residence (AKA "SFR")	A stick-built house which is detached (no common walls with other houses).
Special Assessments	Additional taxes or HOA fees, above the regular fees, charged to the property owner.
Standard Forms	Contract and disclosure templates which are used by many REALTORS®.
Starter Home	The first home that is purchased by home buyers, which may not be the best, the biggest, or their dream home.
Structural Condition	The quality of the house frame, including foundation, floors, roof, and walls.

Subject To (AKA Contingent Upon)	Certain conditions that must be fulfilled in order for the purchase to proceed.
Table Funding	Where all parties gather around the closing table as the loan document signing, loan funding, and closing happens all at once. This is a typical closing procedure for certain states.
Tax Deductions	Expenses that can be deducted from your income tax bill.
Tax-Deductible	An expense or a credit that you can report on your annual tax return, in order to lower your taxes due.
Title Company	A company that researches and guarantees title ownership for the new buyer with a title insurance policy.
Title Insurance	A policy that guarantees home buyers they are receiving legitimate title ownership.
Title Vesting / Vesting Of Title	The legal ownership of the house and how that ownership is held.
Twin Home	A semi-detached house which shares 1 common wall with another house. Each house is separately owned by different owners.
Under Contract	Both buyer and seller have come to a mutual agreement on price & terms, and signed a purchase contract. They are locked into a contract so the house is NOT available for purchase by other buyers.
Underwriting / Loan Underwriting	Mortgage lender's department will approve your loan, they must examine all of your documents and you must meet their strict criteria.
Value / Valuation	How much a house is worth (NOT the same as Asking Price or List Price)

Values	Moral values are ideals incorporated into your family, such as hard work, being debt-free, contributing to charities, generous giving, faith in God, saving money, and community participation.
Walk-Through Inspection (AKA Verification of Property Condition)	When the buyers do their final walk-through before closing, they sign a form to verify its condition.
Will	A legal written directive to be implemented after you die, which tells your heirs and the court what your wishes are.
Wire	Funds which are transferred to a bank account electronically.
Wish List	A buyer's list of features and requirements for a house purchase.
Zero-Down Loan	A loan that does not require a down payment from the buyer, such as a VA loan.

Acronym Definitions

1003	Loan application form from Freddie Mac
4C	Acceleration clause; alienation clause; due-on-sale clause
ABI	Assignment of Beneficial Interest
ABR	Accredited Buyer's Representative (designation from National Association of REALTORS®)
AEA	American Escrow Association
AITD	All Inclusive Trust Deed
ALTA	American Land Title Association
APN	Assessor's Parcel Number (tax ID number)
APR	Annual Percentage Rate
ARM	Adjustable Rate Mortgage
ASHI	American Society of Home Inspectors
AVID	Agent Visual Inspection Disclosure form (form from California Association of REALTORS®)
BA	Buyer's Agent (AKA "SA")
BIA	Buyer Inspection Advisory (form from California Association of REALTORS®)
BK	Bankruptcy
BRE	Bureau of Real Estate (state licensing agency)
CalFIRPTA	California Real Estate Withholding Guidelines
CAMB	California Association of Mortgage Brokers
C/C	Certified Copy
CAR	California Association of REALTORS®
CC&R	Covenants, Codes, and Restrictions

CD	Closing Disclosure
CDA	Commission Disbursement Authorization
CEA	California Escrow Association
CEO	Certified Escrow Officer
CFP	Certified Financial Planner (designation)
ChFC	Chartered Financial Counselor (designation)
CID	Common Interest Development
CLTA	California Land Title Association
CMA	Comparable Market Analysis
COE	Close of Escrow
CP	Community Property
CPA	Certified Public Accountant
CREIA	California Real Estate Inspection Association
DU	Desktop Underwriting (loan approval)
CRV	Certificate of Reasonable Value
CFPB	Consumer Financial Protection Bureau
CSEO	Certified Senior Escrow Officer
DOC	Department of Corporations
DOI	Department of Insurance
DRE	Department of Real Estate (state licensing agency)
DTT	Documentary Transfer Tax
EI	Escrow Instructions
EIC	Escrow Institute of California
EMD	Earnest Money Deposit check
Enjoa	Electronic Notary Journal of Official Acts

EO	Escrow Officer
EOI	Evidence Of Insurance
eSIGN	Electronic Signatures in Global and National Commerce Act
F/C	Free and Clear (property owned outright, without liens or other encumbrances)
FDIC	Federal Deposit Insurance Corporation
FHA	Federal Housing Administration (government agency that underwrites / guarantees mortgage loans)
FHLMC	Federal Home Loan Mortgage Corporation
FIRPTA	Foreign Investment Real Property Tax Act
FNMA	Federal National Mortgage Association
FSBO	For Sale By Owner (house for sale)
FTB	Franchise Tax Board
GD	Grant deed
GFE	Good Faith Estimate (mortgage loan form)
GI	General Index
GP	General Partner
GRI	Graduate REALTOR® Institute (designation from National Association of REALTORS®)
HCD	Housing Community Development
HOA	Home Owners Association
HUD	U.S. Department of Housing and Urban Development (government agency)
HUD-1	Standard real estate settlement form for federally regulated mortgage loans
HW	Homeowners warranty

HWCPROS	Husband and Wife as Community Property with Right Of Survivorship
HWJT	Husband and Wife as Joint Tenants
InterNACHI	International Association of Certified Home Inspectors
IRS	Internal Revenue Service
JT	Joint Tenants
L&V	Legal & Vesting
LA	Listing Agent (real estate agent representing the Seller)
LC	Late Charge
LLC	Limited Liability Company
LOE	Letter Of Explanation (mortgage loan form)
LP	Limited Partner
LTV	Loan To Value
MBA	Mortgage Banker's Association
MERS	Mortgage Electronic Registration System
MIP	Mortgage Insurance Premium
MLS	Multiple Listing Service
MMA	Money Market Account
MMI	Monthly Mortgage Insurance
NACA	Neighborhood Assistance Corporation of America (non-profit organization)
NAHI	National Association of Home Inspectors
NAR	National Association of REALTORS®
NNA	National Notary Association
NOD	Notice Of Default
NOT / NOTS	Notice of Trustee Sale

P&L	Profit and Loss (financial statement from business owners)
PCOR	Preliminary Change of Ownership Report (form filed at County)
PDF	Portable Document Format
PITI	Principal, Interest, Taxes, and Insurance
PIQ	Property In Question
PMI	Private Mortgage Insurance
P/O	Payoff
POA	Power of Attorney
POC	Paid Outside of Closing (expenses not paid through the escrow process)
PPI	Prepaid Interest
POF	Proof of Funds
PR	Preliminary Report (title report)
PRIA	Property Records Industry Association
PUD	Planned Unit Development
QC	Quitclaim Deed
REIT	Real Estate Investment Trust
REO	Real Estate Owned (bank owned property)
RESPA	Real Estate Settlement Procedures Act
RPA-CA	Residential Purchase Agreement and Joint Escrow Instructions (form from California Association of REALTORS®)
SA	Selling Agent (agent representing the Buyer) – AKA "BA"
SFR	Single Family Residence
SI	Statement of Identity form (AKA Statement of Information) from title company

TC	Tenants in Common
TD	Trust Deed
TILA	Truth In Lending Act
TO	Title Officer
TRID	Truth In Lending Disclosure form
Ttee	Trustee
UCC	Uniform Commercial Code
UETA	Uniform Electronic Transaction Act
USDA	U.S. Department of Agriculture (government agency that administers mortgage loans)
VA	U.S. Department of Veterans Affairs (government agency that underwrites/guarantees mortgage loans)
VOD	Verification of Deposit
VOE	Verification Of Employment (mortgage loan form)
VOF	Verification Of Funds (mortgage loan form)
VOI	Verification Of Income (mortgage loan form)
VOM	Verification of Mortgage
VOR	Verification Of Rent Paid (mortgage loan form)
VP	Verification of Property Condition (form from California Association of REALTORS®)
WOP	With Other Property
X	Escrow
XEI	Exchange Escrow Instructions
YSP	Yield Spread Premium

CONCLUSION

Thank you for tuning in to brush up on lingo and learn the real estate terms for house features. We wish you much success in your career... please continue keeping the dream of homeownership alive!

Author Bio

Regina P. Brown is a California Real Estate Broker, licensed since 1988. Her passion is helping families create their legacy through financial education. She offers real estate seminars and consults with clients one-on-one. Because she has experienced 2 full real estate economic cycles, she has learned how to successfully solve many challenging situations. Ms. Brown is a strong advocate for families, consumers, and her clients. Her mission is to:

- Elevate the level of professionalism for real estate and mortgage industry professionals
- Educate consumers, be an advocate, and help bring positive change to our economic system
- Assist families to increase their financial knowledge, economic independence, and wealth freedom through individual counseling and published resources

My mission is to help Americans become financially stable. I believe that homeownership is a critical cornerstone of their financial plan for the future, and the basis for our economy stability.

I applaud you for embracing the humble, yet noble career of a real estate professional. Whether you are a licensed agent, inspector, appraiser, mortgage lender, contractor, or home stager, your work is vital to our country's economy. Your services are essential to your clients' success. Keep performing high quality work and know that you are making a significant impact and contributing to a better America!

About Our Company

RealtyPro Advisor is a training company that offers live advanced professional courses for real estate agents. Interested in real estate training? Look for our online courses at www.RealtyProAdvisor.com and additional professional resources at www.QueenBeePublisher.com

Other Books

We hope you enjoyed our newest version of **Learn the Lingo of Houses:** Reference of Real Estate Terms for Today's Industry Professionals. Check out these other resources.

Premier book from author Regina P. Brown:

Buy Your First Home: A Basic Step-by-Step Guide for First Time Home Buyers book in the following formats: Paperback, eBook, Audio, Online course, and Hard cover book.

Other books, online trainings, and resources from Queen Bee Publisher, Inc.:

Create Your Custom eBook in 1 Day: Share Your Message, Earn Money, & Reach Millions

Break Through Writer's Block: Invigorate Your Mind, Generate New Ideas, & Voice Your Authentic Message Powerfully

Lease a Commercial Business Building: Small Business Owners and Entrepreneurs — Negotiate Your Best Deal

Super Sales Strategies: Customer Service Reference for Retailers

Kids, Open Your Art Shop Today: Create & Sell Your Handmade Crafts

Made in the USA
Lexington, KY
26 May 2016